THIS IS
CRUISING

THIS IS
CRUISING

Second edition

DAS SLEIGHTHOLME

SHERIDAN HOUSE

Second Edition 1989

Copyright © United Nautical Publishers SA, Basel 1988

ISBN 0 911378 88 X

First published
in the United States of America 1989 by
Sheridan House Inc.
145 Palisade Street
Dobbs Ferry, NY 10522

First Edition 1976

Photographs courtesy of Yachting Monthly p30,
Patrick Roach p35, 53, 65, 75, 125, 129
Charles Stock p40, 115, John Kay p101
Barry Pickthall p13, 21, 97
Nick Rains p73
Rick Tomlison p78, 159
Julia Middelmann p91, 105
Alastair Black p133, 137, 150
Avon Inflatables Ltd p143, 155

Illustrations by Peter A G Milne and Mike Collins

Filmset in Great Britain
Printed in Italy

Contents

The Cruising Sailboat

When *This is Sailing*, the first colour book from United Nautical Publishers, passed the quarter million mark of sales in nine languages, it was less of a compliment to the book, than to the phenomenon of yachting as an international sport.

By using colour on every page—drawn by Peter Milne under the direction of Richard Creagh-Osborne—it dug into the practicalities and the feeling of sailing in a way that had unarguably never before been attained on paper. *This is Sailing* used a modern lightweight centreboarder to teach how to sail expertly, but not everyone has this type of boat. All over the world sailors are moving up to—or starting from scratch in—cruisers. These are not cruisers of the old school with baggywrinkle and meat safes, but usually glass fibre, invariably Bermudian sloop rigged, probably under 30 ft or 10 metres and with berths for a family of four or five.

This is the boat which you are going to learn to sail and handle well in the following pages. By sailboat cruising is meant being confident and skilled in moving on the water with family or friends, in light winds and strong, in good visibility and bad, by day and by night. Nor does cruising always imply voyaging or even passage making: here the concern is to handle the cruiser properly whether leaving a marina berth for a few minutes to get some fuel or preparing for a three-week cruise to a foreign shore.

The colour graphics have two major advantages. First, the techniques recommended in the diagrams are vivid: indeed the pictures will speak to you direct, with the words sometimes only there as assistance. Second, it has been possible to reproduce closely cruising situations: for there are few photographs of cruising at sea. If your experience is limited, you can be assured that before long you will come across the very scene that has been described here.

Section by section

The mechanics of sailing have been discussed in *This is Sailing*, but on board a cruising sailboat free to drift on the water you are on a wholly different platform from an open unbal-

lasted centreboarder in the same circumstances. A book about cruising must begin with this point. Des Sleightholme's colour picture scheme then considers the cruiser's qualities and what they imply when moving along the water under sail and power—hull and sail balance, stiffness, windage, pitching, propeller effects, turning in breeze and calm. One really can take one's boat out—book in hand—and try these experiments.

On page 24 you begin to meet objects other than water, hard objects like quaysides and marina berths. So the author goes on to deal with 'Stopping' and how to keep away from danger. Only then can preparations for sailing begin and discussion of the most effective drills in various manoeuvres.

Longer passages are implied around page 74 where crew considerations emerge, then passage planning, navigational and weather preparation and tidal strategy.

What do you see when you make your landfall? The answers to this question cover those pages which some will find the most valuable part of the book. Des Sleightholme has uniquely developed over the years the art of graphically representing 'navigation by eye'. Here the technique is illustrated in colour which has not before been possible. The unpleasant but anticipated situations of fog, bad weather and even rescue from a yacht are in the closing pages.

And afterwards

Sailing and especially cruising, breaks down international barriers and this book has already done so as well. Because as you read it, sailing men overseas are looking at exactly the same visual presentations, though the words are in eight other languages—and being used in more than eight other countries, particularly the English, French and Spanish versions. Even after the words have been read, the diagrams and cruising scenes, aided by either imagination or hindsight, can be used again to envisage variations on fresh aspects of sailboat cruising.

UNITED NAUTICAL PUBLISHERS

Know your boat

To the sailor there is just sheer pleasure in being afloat on the water. This pleasure can be savoured best in the ballasted cruising yacht. In such a boat on a mooring, even in a marina berth, the boat pulls and moves according to wind and current: this constant movement, or potentiality for movement is probably a major contribution to the 'on board' feeling.

But knowledge of the boat begins with learning to harness the pull and movement to make the yacht do what is required. Sails, engine, rudder, keel, the action of wind on hull and structure all play their part, whether the skipper wants it or not. Sails can be lowered or engine switched off but the others always have to be taken into account. Before trying to go places, it becomes worthwhile to analyse the boat's behaviour to sea and wind regardless of sails and engine. Sometimes when the wind on the mast blows her head off, one wishes that the mast was not there at all, but it is and has to be remembered and its effect anticipated.

Hauled ashore on dry land (or dried out after running aground!) is the only time the boat is motionless. A boat never ceases to move, even when moored. Unmoored, she drifts with the current **A** or drifts with the wind **B**, she swings, bobs, rolls and pitches, or she is given forward motion so that she can be steered, or motion astern steering with the rudder reversed.

According to her hull shape, windage, rig and her manoeuvrability – her size or her type – she will be easier or harder to handle under power or sail. Learning the characteristics of one's own boat is the first step in learning to handle her smartly.

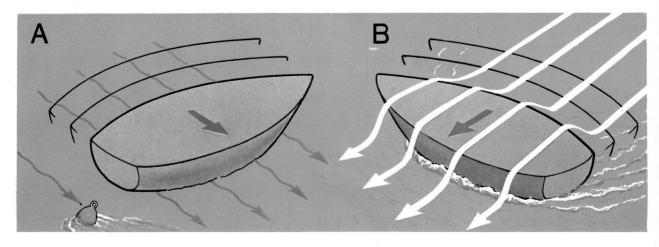

(1) She may have a long keel or a fin-and-skeg, a small mainsail with a short foot plus a large headsail, or she may have the opposite. (2) Her hull may have a canoe, a counter or a transom stern – a variety of rudders. (3) She may be of light displacement and low wetted surface with a fin ballast keel or her hull may be 'all boat' with a long keel and considerable wetted surface area. (4) Likewise her shape and area on the waterline may vary from (a) full with little overhang at bow and stern to (b) fine, (c) powerful and buoyant aft or (d) beamy but fine at bow and stern. In every case not only will the handling characteristics be different but they will change according to the force of the wind and the heeling of the hull.

Drifting behaviour

If allowed to drift with rudder free, a sailing cruiser tends to 'seek the wind' with her stern **A**, but her attitude may vary from almost beam-on to stern to wind. She may wallow straight down wind or she may make a certain amount of headway.

It may be possible to steer her down wind under bare spars **B** and retain good control or there may be very little control. Knowing what can be done may someday get you out of a tricky situation.

With the rudder free to swing she may just lie solidly beam-on or she may 'hunt' around, **C**, drifting slowly or even quite rapidly to leeward according to hull shape and windage. Long keeled hulls **D** tend to drift more consistently than short keeled craft, but not invariably so – you must find out. You must also find out how she will lie if the tiller is lashed amidships or to leeward. All this knowledge of the boat will soon become significant.

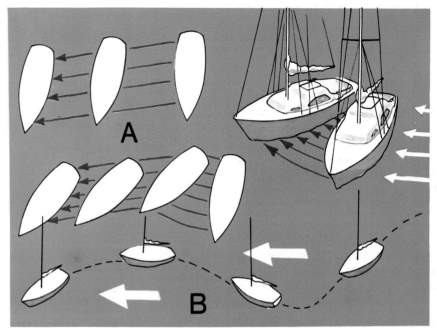

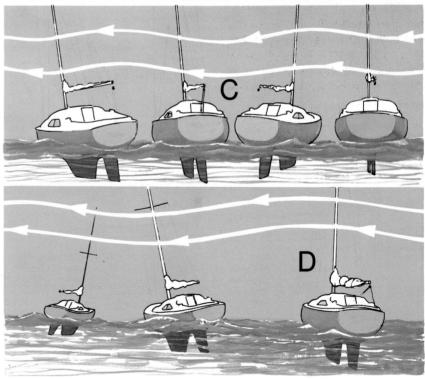

Letting go of the helm

Under sail, a boat has different characteristics. If we let go of the tiller when lying closehauled **E** she may continue to sail herself, luffing or bearing away a little in the wind puffs or **F** she may simply luff herself head to wind, tack herself and lie hove-to with jib a'back. She may even display lee helm characteristics and do the complete opposite, bearing away as in **G** instead of luffing and perhaps even gybing.

According to wind strength and the sails carried, each boat will vary in character and behaviour. From light breeze to strong, storm jib to big genoa, an owner will discover new differences in balance and he will learn to anticipate them.

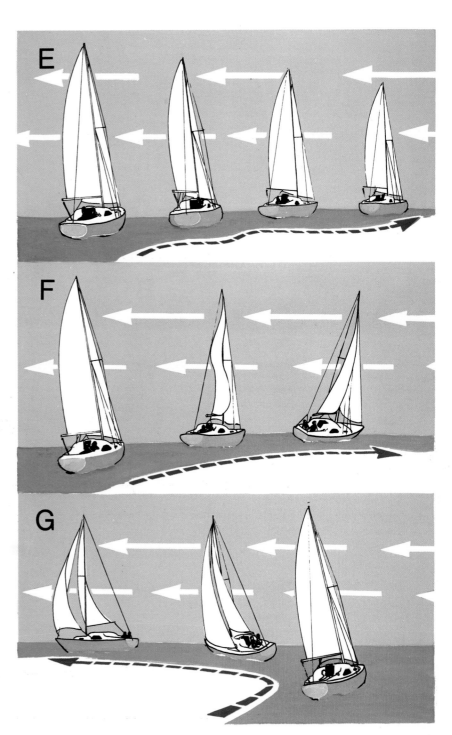

Letting go of the helm

If the helm is released when reaching with the mainsail well freed **A** she may luff and lie with sails a'shake or tack herself and lie with jib a'back. Or if under a very large genoa she could pay off downwind instead. When running wing and wing (main and headsail on opposite sides) **C**, she would probably behave as in **B** (left) – but she might also gybe.

Under headsail or mainsail only her behaviour **D** will alter completely, as it would under deep reefed main and working jib. It is important to know by how much it will alter.

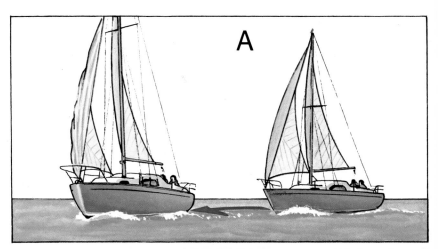

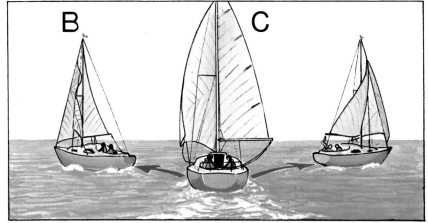

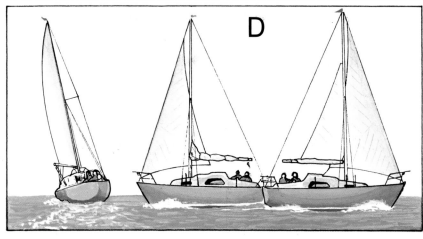

A worthy pipedream for the cruising enthusiast. This cutter, for all her daintiness, has the look of a hard weather boat. Her mainsail can be deeply reefed and the twin headsails allow her to be snugged down to an all-inboard rig, with a storm jib set on the inner stay. A booming-out spar stows up the mast for use, perhaps with a cruising chute, in kinder weather.

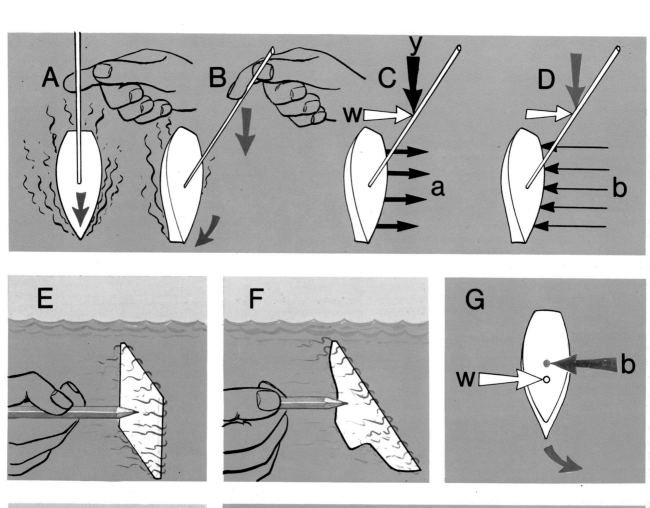

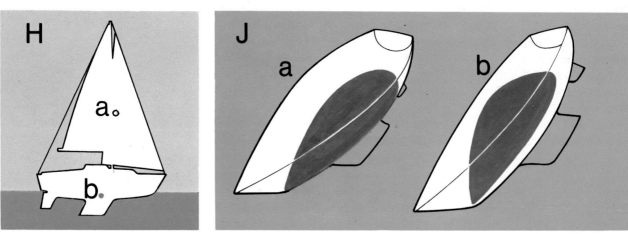

Hull and sail balance

When heeled a boat will not be as simple to handle as when cruising upright.

(Left) **A**. Sails apply forward pressure to a mast but when heeled it passes outside the hull centreline **B** and tends to turn the boat into the wind. In **C** we have drive (y), side pressure (w) and side drift (a). In **D** drift is resisted by water pressure. (b)

E. Imagine a plate pushed at its exact centre of lateral resistance – or similarly a hull profile **F**. If we find the exact centre of effort for the sails (COE) and contrive a rig in which it comes just ahead of the hull centre of lateral resistance, it will balance out the luffing tendency. In G (w) is the COE and (b) is the CLR.

H. This is how the design might appear with COE (a) and CLR (b). J. As the hull (a) heels, the shape of the waterline immersed changes, (b) thus a short beamy hull presents a less symmetrical shape than a long, fine keel.

K is typical of the imbalance when sailing a small cruiser with weather helm. She is trying to push up to windward and continuous pull on the tiller is necessary by the helmsman.

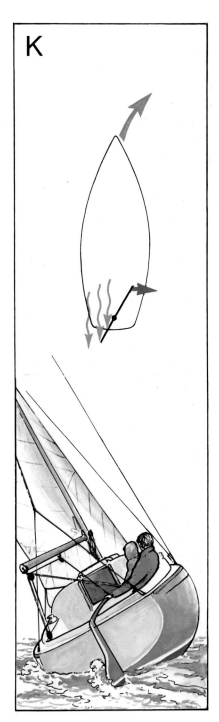

15

Windward ability

Could you beat off a lee shore in a gale? Boat **A** certainly could not. Under sail alone her excessive leeway and lack of sail power turn her close-hauled course into a broad reach. Use of engine also might make only slight improvement.

B Few small cruisers are wrecked in this way though. Wind direction is seldom constant for long and *any* shift makes one tack a better offshore one than the other. Cruiser (a) cannot weather the headland but a wind shift (thick arrows) used to advantage (b) allows her to point further offshore and weather the headland.

The experienced skipper is constantly alert for wind shifts and wastes no time in using them, knowing well enough that the wind may shift back yet again. He also knows how and when to combine engine with sail power.

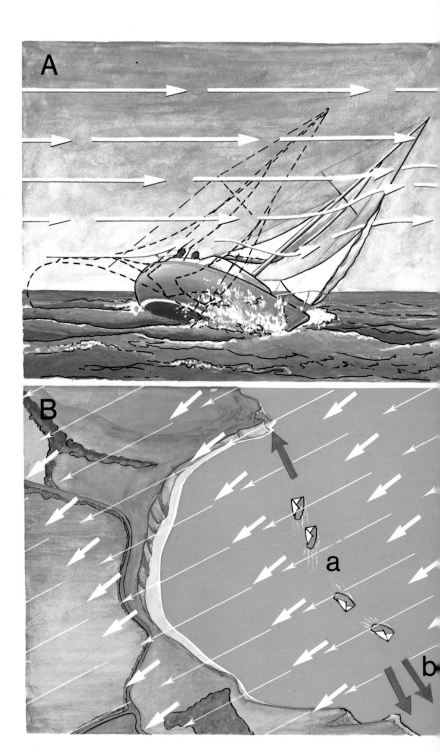

Auxiliary power

Both boats **C** and **D** have 40hp engines but whereas the planing boat **C** uses most of her power, heavy hull **D** wastes much of it in propeller slip or cavitation. She needs a slower turning, larger and more coarsely pitched propeller to give 'bite'.

Boat **E**, a sailing racer, only needs a small power unit for harbour work but boat **F**, of heavy displacement, needs solid thrust for head wind slogging – a more powerful engine with 3-blade propeller slow-turning for a coarse bite.

Motors themselves, like cruisers, are a compromise. Propeller drag, while sailing, spoils performance but propeller power for motor-sailing demands a propeller which is of correct size and design for maximum efficiency. Without this, a propeller may produce maximum boat speed in a calm sea **G** but lack drive, due to cavitation, in a head sea **H**.

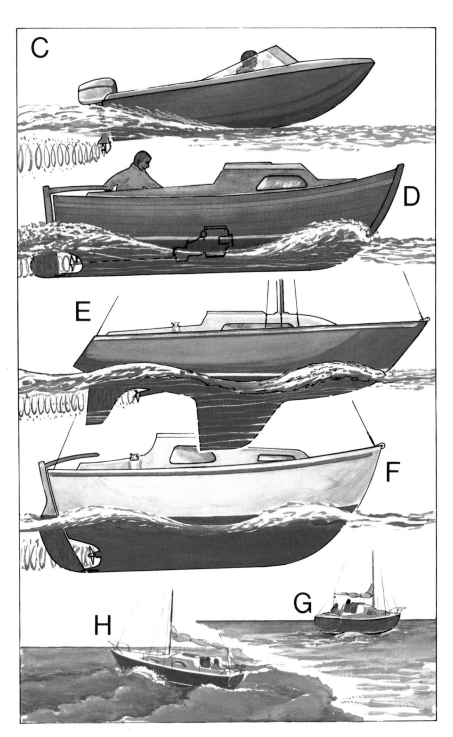

Propeller
side effect

Water density increases rapidly with depth. The blades of a spinning propeller, biting denser water in the bottom half of their circle than in the upper half, exert a side-paddle effect.

Imagine a box with a wheel at one end **E**. If the wheel is turned as shown, the end of the box will move to the right. A righthanded or clockwise turning propeller tends to kick the stern of the boat to the right as well as driving forward **F** – to a lesser extent of course. Slow-turning large diameter propellers have pronounced side effect.

G. With a stern bias towards starboard the boat tends to turn her bows to port when going ahead. With engine astern though (propeller turning left handed) the reverse happens – stern to port, bows swinging to starboard. The pivot point red dot moves aft when going astern. Note the rudder banging itself hard over due to water pressure when making sternway. (Green arrows, bottom right.)

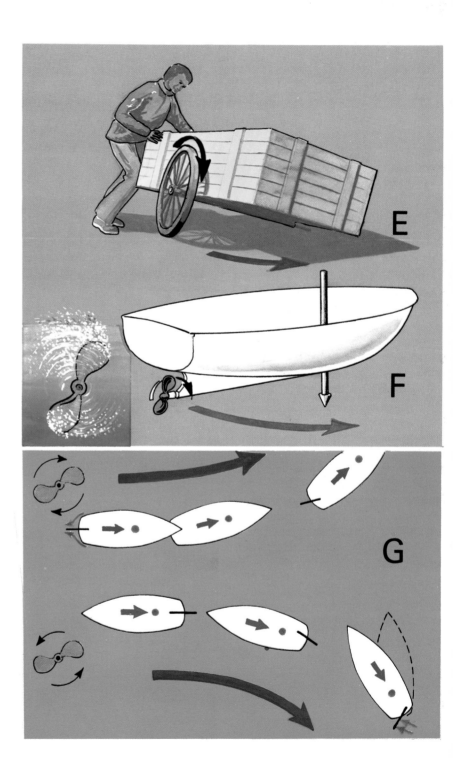

Handling under power (calm)

Propeller side effect can be used in manoeuvring. With a righthanded propeller a circle to port will be tighter than one to starboard (the opposite with a lefthanded propeller) **A-B** shows the effect of a righthand propeller of considerable side-kick. In reverse she will turn her stern to port **C** but she may not turn it to starboard **D**. (Opposite effect for left handed propeller).

Auxiliaries can seldom be turned tightly by alternately going ahead and astern and relying upon helm assistance, but short, hard bursts ahead on full helm, alternated with short, hard bursts astern (no helm change) to check headway often work. The modern auxiliary cruiser will however usually turn in about $1\frac{1}{2}$ lengths, engine ahead on full helm, **E**. Note how the stern swings outwards.

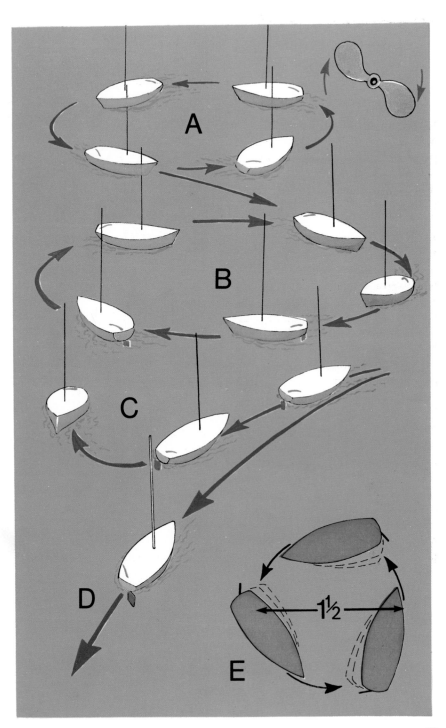

Handling under power (fresh breeze)

Without sails or engine, no headway, a boat will always swing her stern to windward, bows downwind (1-2-3). This 'wind-seeking' or weathercock tendency is at the root of all power handling in a fresh breeze.

In **F1** to **F4** the cruiser with the wind abeam can be turned *downwind* easily and tightly because her stern wants to seek the wind. In **G1** to **G4** an attempt to turn her bows into the wind is more difficult because it is contrary to the wind-seeking rule. If, additionally, she has pronounced propeller side-kick to starboard (in this case), a turn into wind to starboard might prove impossible.

Some craft, due to windage and side-kick, can only be turned one way into the wind. Many need full helm and full engine to turn them into wind.

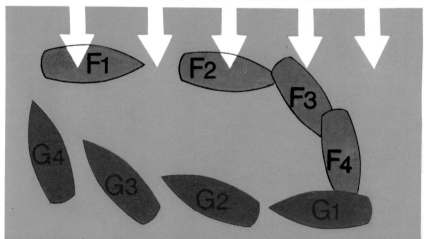

Conditions are ideal for manoeuvring in harbour as this yacht leaves her berth and turns into the wind towards the harbour entrance. The same scene on a windy day could be very different, although leaving a berth is usually far simpler than entering one.

Tight turning
(wind abeam)

Not all cruisers will turn in just over a length; it also needs confidence to attempt a full-ahead turn in a confined space. The blue yacht is making an ahead-astern turn. At 1, 2, 3 she goes ahead turning upwind and then goes astern (4, 5) using her stern-kick to port (right-handed propeller), finally going ahead again (5, 6).

The red cruiser uses a different tactic, she goes ahead (1–2) and then makes a stern board (3) utilizing both her astern kick to port and the wind-seeking tendency to take her well up wind (4–5). She then goes full ahead on full starboard rudder (6, 7).

Much depends upon room available, whether there is also a current to allow for and the individual performance of the boat. In an emergency don't just go full ahead and hope and don't rely upon the stopping power of the engine astern.

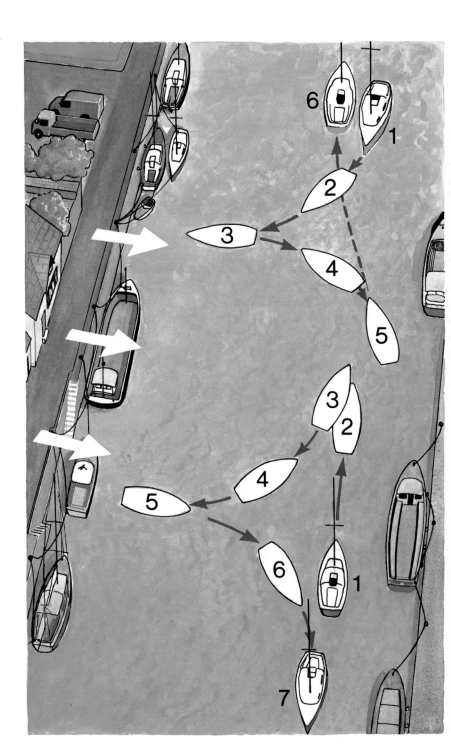

Tight turns
(wind ahead or astern)

The blue cruiser (1, 2, 3) turns to starboard because her right handed propeller will then give her stern its kick to port as she goes astern. This starts her stern wind-seeking, (4), she then goes ahead again, (4–5).

The red cruiser with the wind astern has a more difficult turn to make. She hugs the river bank in order to have maximum room for a turn to port – her tightest turn with a right-handed propeller. She then turns on full helm, (2, 3, 4, 5) with plenty of power, but her helmsman must gauge whether she'll make it before she fouls the anchored purple yacht.

In a strong wind and with a boat which is slow to turn it may be better to reach position 3 at slow speed and then open the engine to full power with the rudder hard over in an attempt to kick the stern round. Failing this she must anchor, swing head to wind and then proceed, lifting the anchor as she goes.

Going alongside

A. Assuming a kick of stern to port with engine astern, an approach (1–4) head to wind, allows a slow approach with stern slewing towards the wall as the engine is given a burst astern. If circumstances dictated a *starboard* side to wall berthing, the stern kick would be a hindrance and the engine would be used to slow her more gradually.

B. Current ahead, wind astern. She must stem the current, going astern to slow and slew her stern in. Rapid work with mooring lines is needed, if wind and current are together, berth heading into both.

C. With wind abeam as shown, beware of the bows falling to leeward as she slows and loses steerage way. In the final approach steer off the wall a shade, letting her blow in bodily.

Berthing in marinas

D. In a strong cross wind and making for a berth, boats **E1** and **E2** will need very different handling, due to their different turning ability and power handling characteristics. You must know your boat.

Some craft will be sufficiently manoeuvrable to be taken straight in but others may get out of control as soon as steerage way drops and their bows will pay off downwind. If the manoeuvre is plainly not working out as planned, it is usually safer to go hard astern out of the berth and make a second attempt. The temptation is to begin an attempt to manoeuvre by going ahead and astern in rapid succession. In such conditions it seldom succeeds.

Marinas

Long keeled boat **A** has played safe, berthing on the end of the finger pier (1–2), securing at (a) for a few moments until stern line is also secured. She is then allowed to drop back, her crew controlling her on her lines (b) until she is berthed (3). Given a big engine and a fast crew she *might* have been taken straight in and stopped astern, if the crew were smartly ashore with lines. The price of error is daunting.

Modern boat **B** is highly manoeuvrable and *might* have been run
straight in, stopped dead on engine
and secured. Such craft are often
very easily handled astern and an
approach (1–2–3) is practicable,
sheering across wind with stern a
little upwind. If making for the leeward berth approaching stern to
wind (**C**) is also possible.

In all cases, crew work with lines
can make or mar any manoeuvre.
Train your crew.

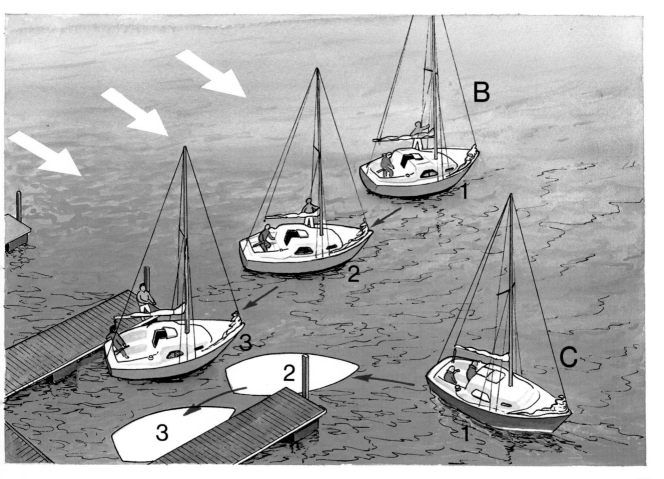

Berthing stern-to

The procedure of anchoring, then manoeuvring stern-first into a berth. **C** With wind abeam, an attempt is foiled by stern swinging upwind. Crew handle her in alongside the already moored yacht. Cruiser **D** has a man detailed to check the out-running anchor cable in order to 'twitch' her bows straight. Cruiser **E**, with good astern control, motors astern straight in.

In strong beam winds, motoring in bows first to secure a long line to the quay, then motoring out stern first will allow the boat to swing up stern to wind. She can then go ahead, lay her anchor and back in under control between anchor cable and stern line.

Remember, in a strong beam wind, the anchors of yachts already moored will be to windward of their berths. Place yours also a little to windward of the vacant berth.

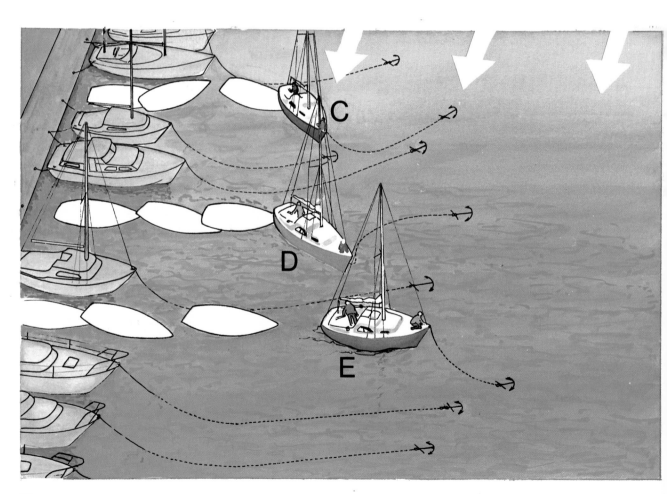

Stopping by going astern

Only practice makes it possible to judge stopping power by going astern. Going full astern as at **A** can cause the stern to swing out of line on the approach, (1–2–3–4), necessitating a burst ahead to correct it. A gradual application of reverse gear, retaining helm control, is usually better. With wind astern she will be sailing in under bare mast.

B With fore knowledge of good astern power when needed though, an approach in neutral, sailing on the mast, then simultaneously going hard astern and securing a stern line (**B** 3–4) may be possible. Faulty crew work could be a hazard. A propeller in reverse gives far less power than it does in forward gear. It may stop her on a calm day but have little effect in a smart following breeze.

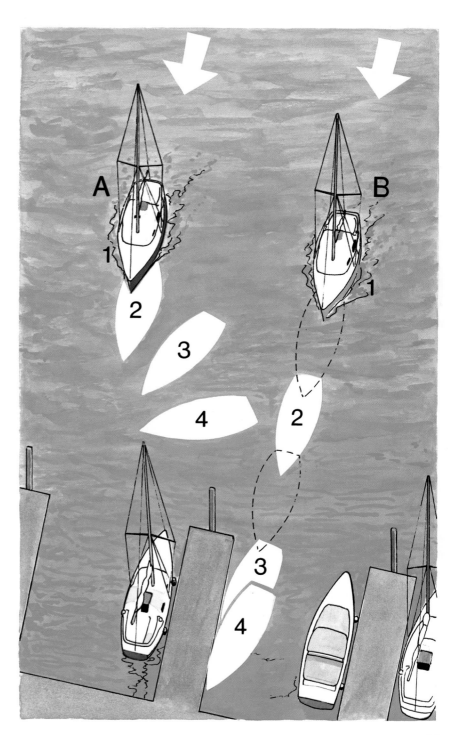

Preparing for sailing

Whether a cruiser goes to sea for a half hour sail or for an extended passage, she must be fully operational and ready to stand up to any emergency. This means that she must be competently crewed and that she must have her full equipment aboard, including charts, navigational instruments and the gear needed for sailing at night.

It is easy to argue that with a quiet day sail in view and the sails, rigging and engine all in good condition, there is no need to equip her with distress signals, food, water, bedding all the essentials for prolonged cruising. Many an owner, out for a short sail, has found himself the victim of circumstance – perhaps on account of a sudden offshore blow combined with a failure of gear – and had to fight his way home in an ill-prepared boat. In a small boat you either go to sea or you stay in harbour and going to sea means going prepared for what the sea can do.

Prior to any sail, no matter how short, an owner should have up-to-date weather information and he should continue to listen to radio forecasts as he goes along. He must also study local conditions and watch his barometer because official forecasts are not always either recent or accurate in local detail.

There must be drinking water in the tanks and a full tank and reserve supply of engine fuel, also warm clothing and oilskins, lifejackets and bedding for all crew.

For the same reasons, boat and engine maintenance should be an on-going practice. The little breakages and weaknesses that accumulate can combine to cause a major fault usually at the worst time and it is unwise to leave them until 'a suitable opportunity' to cope with them occurs. Keep a maintenance log book.

1. Look at the spreaders in case some other boat has been alongside in your absence and caused damage aloft – it could mean the loss of the mast.

2. Check navigation lights and battery regularly.

3. See that anchor and cable a[re] always ready for use.

4. Make sure that rigging screws a[re] properly locked and/or seized.

5. Check that the bilge pump is i[n] working order.

6. Check fuel and reserve tanks a[re] full.

7. Check lifelines are not worn o[r] damaged.

8. Check that the engine is proper[ly] serviced and easy to start.

9. Check that the warps and heav[y] ing lines are ready for use.

10. Check that the lifebuoy is read[y] for instant use complete with light.

11. Check that the distress signals ar[e] up to date and in easy reach.

12. Check that the steering compas[s] has been corrected.

Luffs

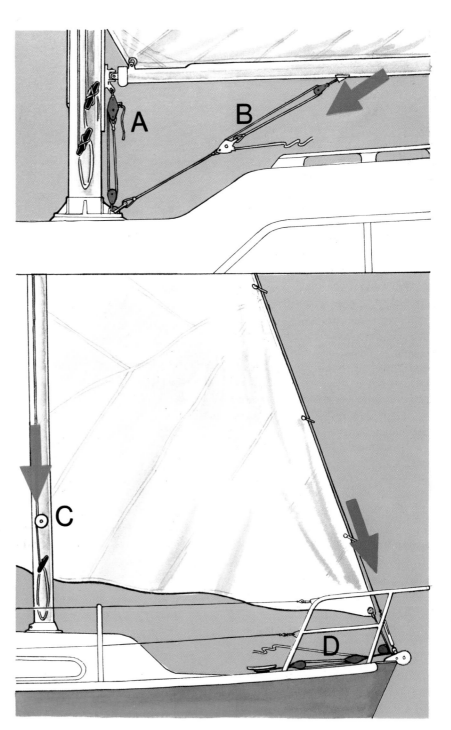

ails are designed to be hauled out rmly along the luff and the foot in rder to put shape into the sail. A ainsail luff may need a tack tackle , if halyard winches are not fitted r in the absence of some other eans of tensioning it. The kicking rap (or boom vang) **B** holds the oom down and reduces mainsail wist.

eadsail luffs can be tensioned by eans of a halyard winch **C** or/and a ck tackle **D**. The fall of this tackle ay be led aft to the cockpit for asier adjustment.

he luff tensions of main and head-ail are varied according to wind rength, being set up hard in fresh reezes and eased away in light airs order to put more shape into the il. They are never allowed to ecome completely slack though. A eadsail with a scalloped luff is a gn of a badly run boat.

Sheeting

Mainsail and headsail must be individually set and trimmed but they must also be regarded as working together as one unit. Correctly trimmed, the airflow over, round and between the sails is smooth and unrestricted. The 'slot' between headsail and mainsail must be kept open and even in order to achieve maximum rig efficiency.

E. Reaching with sails trimmed too flat. Loss of drive and harmful turbulence at back of mainsail.

F. Reaching with the mainsail sheeted too free.

G. Reaching with sails correctly sheeted and working together.

H. A close reach with sails properly trimmed together and the slot working efficiently.

J1. Sheet lead too short resulting in a slack foot and a taut leech.

J2. Sheet lead correctly in line, creating a 90° angle to the luff. Even tensions on foot and leech.

J3. Sheet lead too far aft resulting in a tight foot and a slack leech.

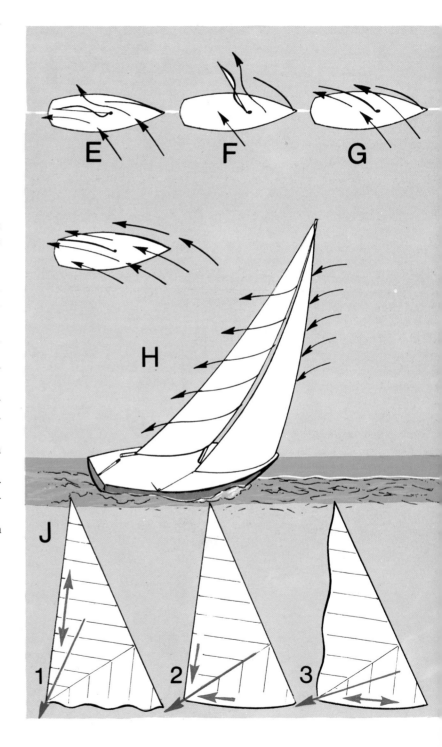

Working on
deck in safety

Constant alertness, good balance and secure footing plus instinctive use of grab points are essential.

A Grab points at: pulpit, harness hook-on wire, shrouds, guard rail, after pulpit, grab rail, forestay, backstay.

B Danger areas where crew is at risk due to being off balance are marked in red. Foredeck, out of reach of mast, rails or forestay; hatch top; cockpit/sidedeck climbing area; after deck.

C shows safest areas (green) where there are adequate grab holds and protection. Beware complacency though. In bad weather more people have gone overboard from the cockpit than from the foredeck.

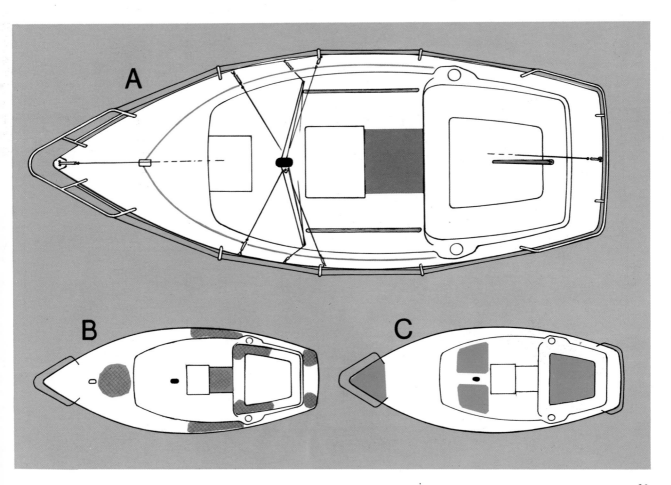

Working on deck in safety

D. A man on the foredeck may be out of grab reach and a harness won't stop him from going overboard. Fixed grab points when going forward or aft should be used, but a (red) line rigged from mast to deck cleat provides extra hold.

To step on wet synthetic sails **E**, which are very slippery, is dangerous and it is safer to kneel or sit **F** in rough weather. The wise man always hooks an arm around any convenient stay when both hands are needed **G**.

'She'll take another inch'. Fast sailing in shelter, no oilskins needed yet. Once at sea it will be a different story and in the wild motion, this winchman would never risk his present position even though he would be wearing a harness. The cockpit, while creating a feeling of security, is a potentially dangerous place when the yacht is heeling and plunging.

Safe sail handling

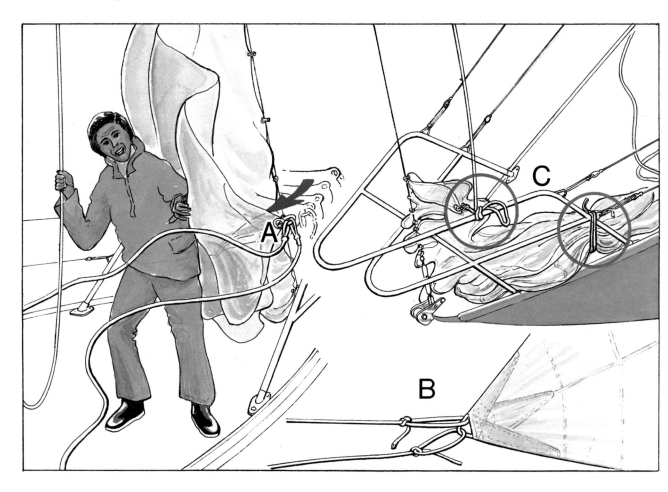

Wind-filled sails represent power which must be controlled by sheet and halyard. Spilling wind sheds power but the flogging sail creates noise and violent movement. Freed from the control of sheets and halyards, sails can balloon and take charge if wind is allowed to fill them. Always stay to windward of a flogging sail, muzzle it quickly or spill the wind out of it, then lash it securely.

A. Shackles used to attach sheets to headsails can cause injury when the sail is flogging. **C**. When lowering a headsail be sure to secure the fall (the halyard end) so that it cannot run aloft, also hitch the head of the sail to the pulpit by its halyard to prevent it riding back up the stay – or better still remove the halyard and snap it on to the pulpit – and lash the sail to the pulpit with a sail-tie until there is time to unhank it. It is safer to attach the

sheets to a sail by making short-up bowlines **B** instead of using shackles or patent clips.

Violent motion in a seaway makes the stowing of a mainsail dangerous. Before a man is allowed to begin stowing the lowered sail be sure to secure the mainsheet properly, hitching the sheet around the block as shown if it is a cam-block type. Failure to do this means a risk of the boom swinging out over the side carrying a crewman with it. In such conditions a safety harness should always be worn.

Never stand upright on the coachroof – kneel or sit. See that the head of the sail is hitched by its halyard to a cleat on the mast so that it cannot balloon up the mast track, torn free by the whipping of the halyard.

The worst conditions for handling and stowing sails are when the wind is astern and there is a rough following sea because the motion will be a wild, rolling lurch and the sails, being attached by their luffs to mast or stay, will be most prone to ballooning. If possible try to come head to wind and lie quietly while sails are being stowed, reefed or changed.

Stowing sails

A headsail can be stowed in its bag **A** while remaining hanked to the stay. Sheets must be disconnected and the halyard either secured or unclipped and snapped on to the pulpit. Bag stowage keeps a sail clean when handling warps or anchor and leaves it ready for instant use. A very temporary stow **B** requires the halyard to be well secured otherwise its jerking will tear the sail free.

Stages in stowing a mainsail. **C** Pull the leech forward to form a bag into which the loose bunt of the sail is bundled. **D** Pull out a fold from the foot and shake the loose sail down, then roll up on to the top of the boom. **E**. Pass sail-ties or gaskets criss-cross and tie.

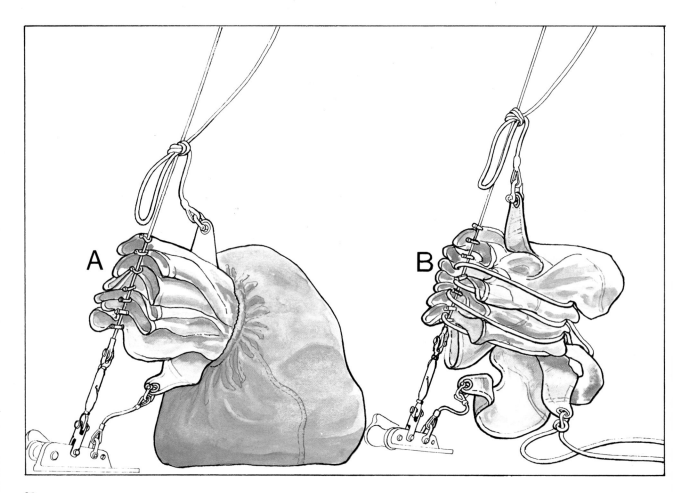

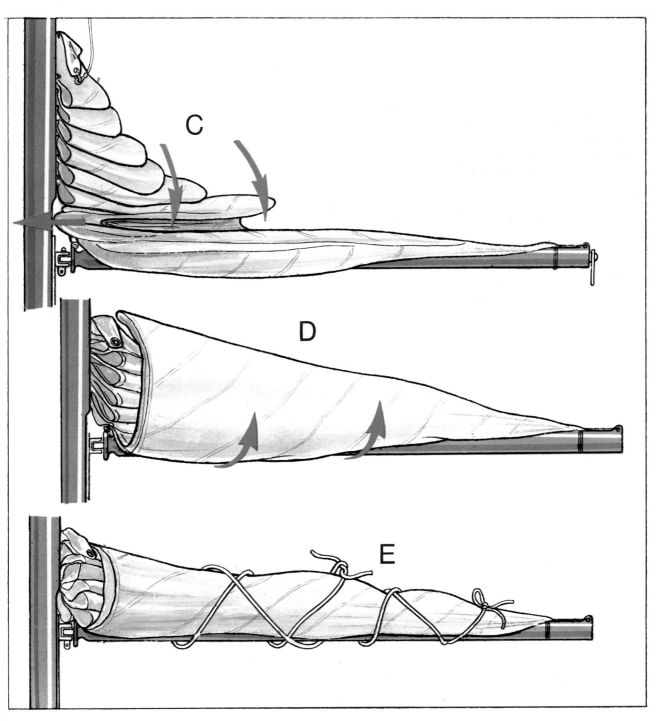

A cruiser race provides good training in sail changing and handling. With a reach apparently about to turn into a close fetch, this crewman is getting ready to set a headsail so that the spinnaker can be lowered in its lee.

Carrying her way

Wind and sea conditions constantly affect the amount of way a boat will carry. At **A** when sails are lowered, she continues to carry her way far down wind, 'sailing' under her bare mast. At **B** however luffing head to wind, the windage of hull and rig bring her to a standstill in perhaps one and a half lengths.

At **C** on a reach, the slackening of the sails by easing sheets slow her at first but as speed drops and the apparent wind comes broader on the beam, lost steerage way causes the bows to pay off and the sails to fill again. **D**. Only luffing will really slow her, or putting helm hard down and freeing the headsail completely.

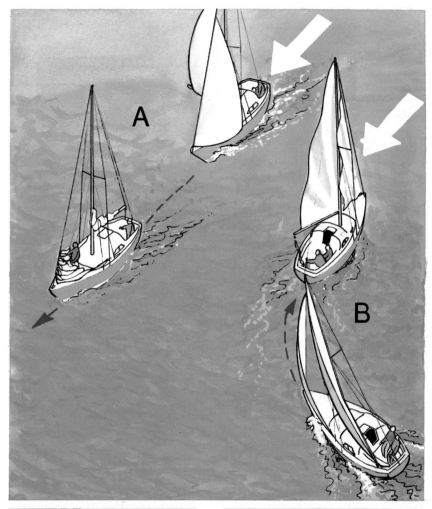

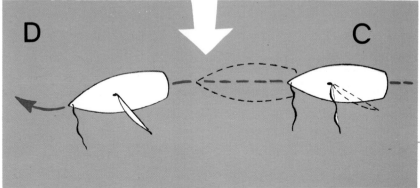

Slowing and stopping

An owner needs to be able to slow down or stop his boat while under sail, to allow time for proper chartwork, for reefing or sail changing, or even to have a meal in comfort. A headsail can be let fly to spill wind completely on any point of sailing, but a mainsail can only be freed off until the boom touches the shrouds **A**. By heading a little into the wind though **B** and by lashing the tiller a'lee both sails can be 'feathered'.

Lying thus with wind abeam **C** the gradual loss of headway brings the apparent wind from forward of the beam further and further aft until the mainsail begins driving again (far left). Thereafter she may drift slowly ahead, luffing herself and paying off by turns.

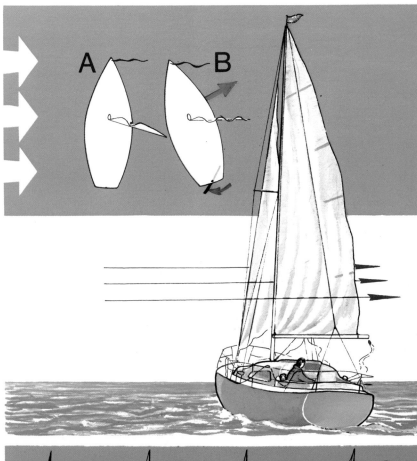

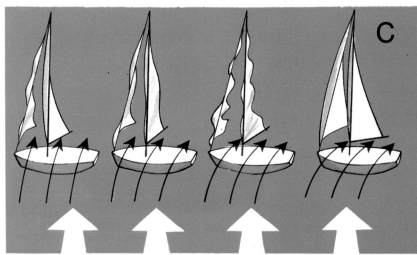

Heaving to with headsail a'back, mainsail sheeted in and tiller lashed a'lee does not always work well in in keeled craft, which may 'hunt' or swerve around **D**. However, with sails trimmed as in **E1** or **E2** the boat should lie quietly. All boats differ and one must experiment.

Heaving-to for lunch in a moderate breeze and doing so as a safety measure in bad weather are very different manoeuvres. In the latter case, mainsail only **F1** or small headsail only **F2** with tiller lashed a'lee may be the only practicable recourse. Rate of drift may be around ? knots at right angles to the wind – much more in bad weather, but boats vary considerably.

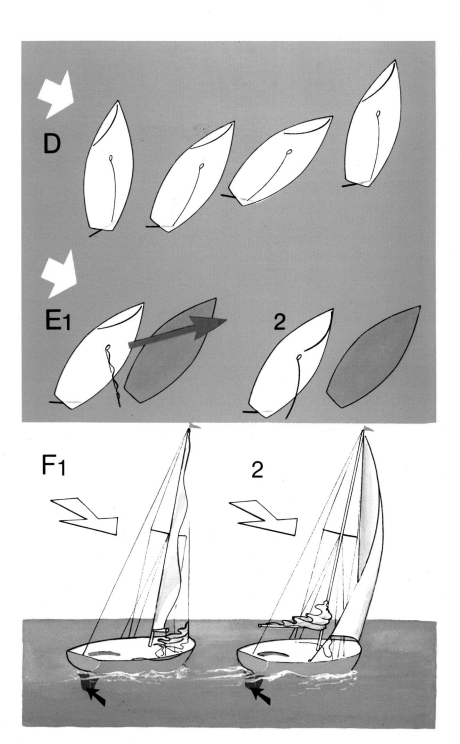

Anchors and anchoring

Anchors in small sailing cruisers should really be a shade heavier than the weight recommended for the size of boat. No anchor can be *too* big, or line *too* long when anchored, but handling the gear on deck can often be a problem. A smaller anchor may hold safely in an ideal seabed but it will soon drag if the ground is soft or if it is too hard for it to penetrate properly, even though it might be quicker to get over the side.

The deeper it can bury the better. A concrete block may at best exert a holding power of its own weight × 1–2 unless deeply buried or exerting suction. A conventional 'fisherman' anchor holds up to 7–10 times its weight on a sandy seabed, but plough and burying type anchors exert a hold of at least their weight × 30 – provided they are able to bury.

In normal weather a cruiser may only exert a few pounds of load but windage, waves, jerking and sheering in bad weather can double and treble the load.

The scope of line paid out is popularly quoted as being a requirement of depth of water × 3 for a chain cable and depth × 5 for rope, but this is an absolute minimum for normal weather only – unless a much heavier anchor is used. A rope line is improved by a short length of chain next to the anchor to assist a horizontal lead. There must be sufficient length of cable aboard to provide a scope of up to × 10, in really bad conditions – possibly even more in bad holding ground. Spare warps of suitable size can be added to the anchor line to increase the scope.

Greater scope will reduce jerking and snubbing but it may also increase the tendency for the cruiser to sheer about. It is the weight of a chain that provides its shock absorbence and the elasticity of nylon warp produces a similar effect. Without this the line may part or the jerks may break out the anchor.

A suitable anchor and a generous scope of cable is a form of insurance.

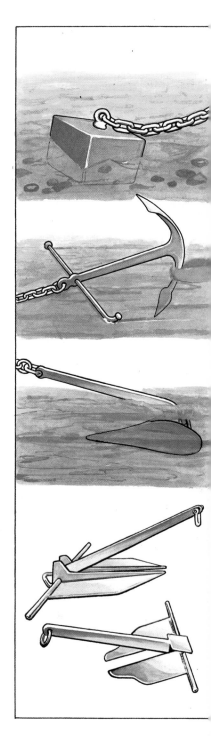

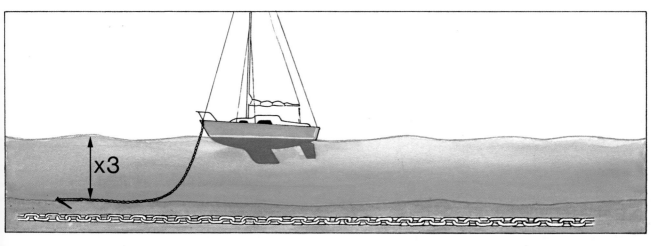

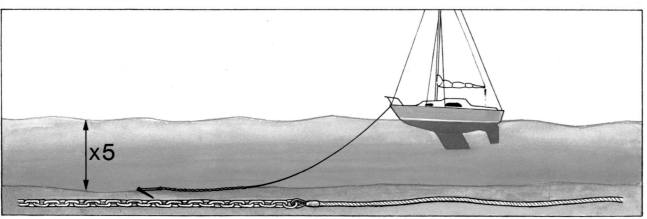

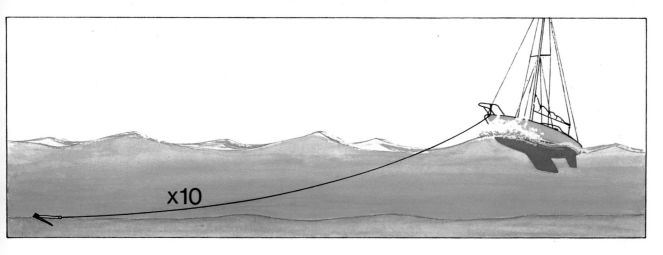

Room to swing

Every vessel at anchor or on a swinging mooring must have a clear arc of swing. The arcs of a number of craft moored or anchored close together may intersect, but provided all craft swing together and to the same extent and in the same direction they will not collide.

They may collide if some are of very different types to their neighbours. A boat with a long, deep keel lies more to the current than to the wind in lighter breezes but a shallow, light hull may do quite the opposite. Mast and hull windage are a big influence and some craft may 'sail' around their anchors when wind and current oppose, while others may simply take a sheer to one side and thereafter lie quietly.

At **A** all are lying to the wind, well separated, but at **B**, with current against wind, they have sheered in various directions, leaving open spaces between them. If a newcomer anchored in these spaces, he would find himself foul of his neighbours when the wind or current changed direction or altered in force.

In order to anchor correctly in crowded waters it is important to try to estimate where the anchors or moorings of nearby craft are positioned, relative to the actual positions of the boats using them.

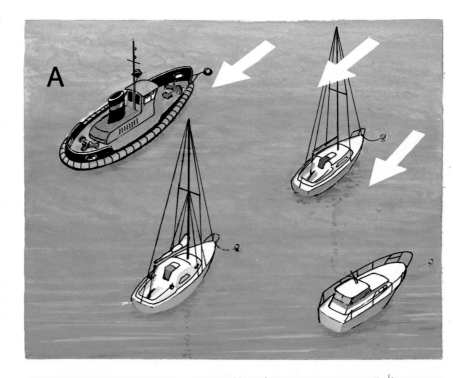

47

Letting go the anchor

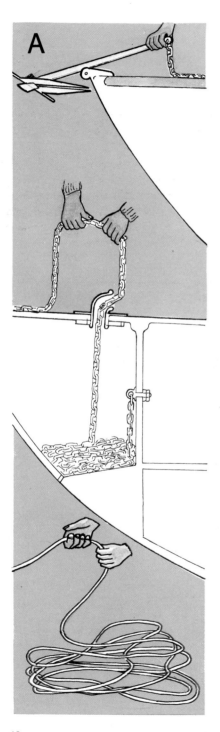

Having decided where the cruiser is to be brought up and therefore where her anchor must be placed in order that she will lie in the position chosen for her, the helmsman must manoeuvre his *bows* to the exact spot for letting go. If the boat is moving too fast, the anchor will not hit the seabed at the spot chosen, neither will it do so if the crew is slow in letting go.

Delay in letting go and/or paying out the cable ruins many good attempts **A**. The anchor should be slung outside the stem and the cable ready overhauled (hauled out of its locker and run back again to free it of kinks). A rope should be 'flaked' (see the sketch) and not coiled if it is to run freely.

B. The cruiser, (1), first circles the anchorage, her skipper sizing up the situation. At (2) he has selected her berth and he takes a sweep in order to be able to round up into the wind for letting go, (3). Time spent in conning an anchorage is never wasted.

C. Be prepared for the bows paying off downwind after letting go. The cruiser luffing (1–2) and letting go will immediately pay off and begin to sail again (3–4). The crew must pay out cable generously or the anchor may be dislodged. Do not snub the anchor until it has scope enough to take an initial hold in the seabed.

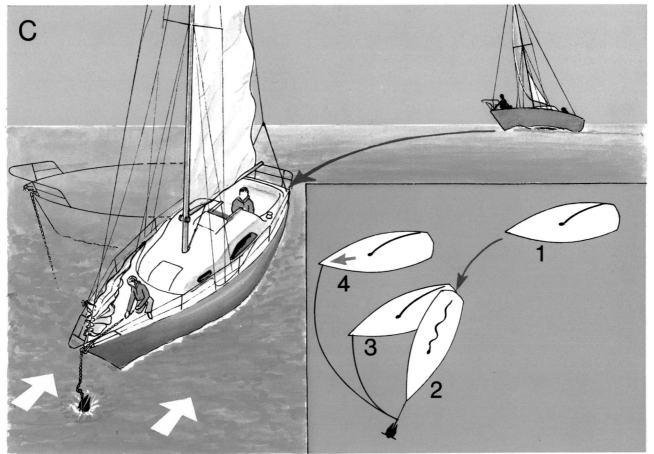

Letting go on a reach

In a narrow channel the cruiser skipper should try to approach his chosen anchorage along the lee side of the channel, easing his sheets in order to slow down. If he carries too much way when he luffs up to let go, his way will make it difficult to judge exactly where his anchor will come to rest. At (1) she has luffed and having let go, (2), she overshoots her anchor, falling back over it, (3) and (4), finally bringing up head to wind at (5). It is important that scope is paid out smartly. It is possible that in falling back over her anchor the chain may disturb it and the boat illustrated has guarded against this by sheering to port with the last of her steerage way, to carry her anchor line clear.

Letting go/Wind against current

A running approach to the anchorage is made, reducing sail to the stage when she may even be sailing over the opposing current under her bare mast. In lighter winds, an approach under headsail only may be the right area of sail. At (1) the cruiser is under headsail, but at (2), to reduce speed still further, she has stowed this also and proceeds under bare pole.

She lets go anchor at (3) and carries her way past it, bringing up at the end of her paid out scope, (4), and then paying off beam to wind, (5) and (6). At this point there may be very little strain on her anchor, the cruiser being held between the forces of current acting on her hull and windage acting upon her rig. According to strengths of wind and current she may then either lie quietly, albeit beam on, or she may begin to sheer about at the end of her cable.

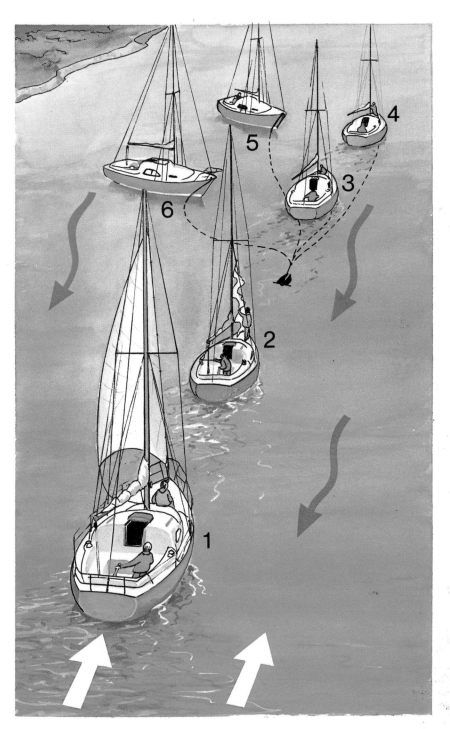

Weighing anchor

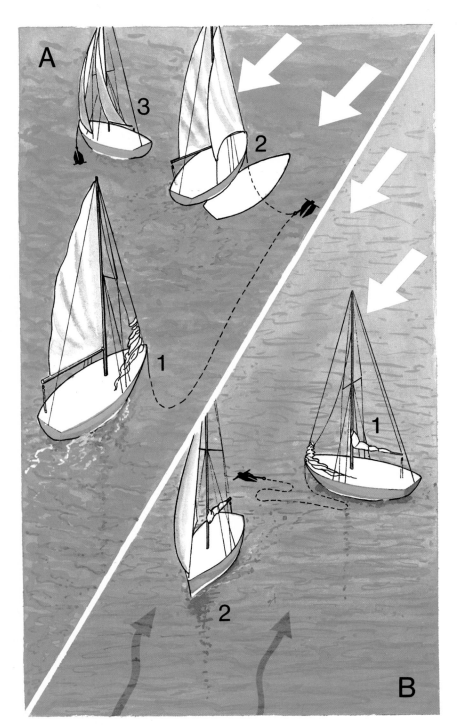

After breaking out the anchor from its hold on the seabed, it may be important to ensure that the cruiser pays off on a particular tack: perhaps only one tack leads clear into safe water. In **A**, at (1), she has her mainsail set and the headsail ready to hoist. At (2), when the cable has been shortened up almost to the point of breaking out the anchor, the headsail is set and backed so that as the anchor breaks out, it will force the boat's head in the desired direction, (3).

B. With wind against current the mainsail cannot be set until she has her anchor clear, otherwise, held by her bow, she will commence sailing around on her anchor. The anchor can be broken out, (1–2) and she can be run off downwind under jib until there is sea room to round up and set the mainsail.

The sheltered anchorage (right) is deceptive. The reefed mainsail suggests that this crew is about to make a short passage, still in shelter, otherwise the dinghy would have been aboard by now. In such rocky surroundings anchoring safely calls for careful selection of seabed from the chart since a rock-strewn holding ground can be tenuous – or the anchor can become foul.

Picking up a mooring

A. With wind against current the correct procedure is to lower the mainsail and approach against the current with wind astern. According to its strength the approach may be made under headsail or under bare mast. Never attempt the pickup under mainsail. The moment the bows are secured to the mooring, the boat will sheer wildly and she may gybe violently.

B. When a current does not have to be allowed for, a broad reaching approach to the buoy is easiest, perhaps under mainsail only to leave the foredeck clear. The mainsail has been freed off to slow her. It is hauled in a little in order to give her more steerage way and it is spilled again near the buoy to slow for the pickup.

With wind and current both together, a closehauled approach and a final short luff to the buoy is the only safe method.

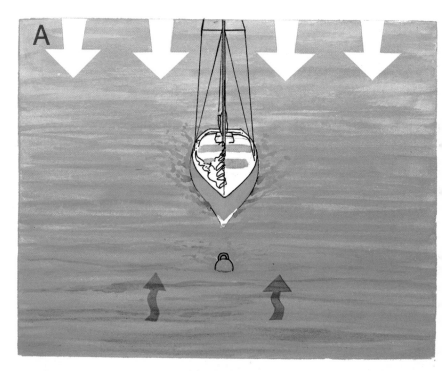

Luffing head to wind in a light breeze **C** may allow way to be carried for several lengths and permit the mooring buoy to be picked up, but the same luff made in strong wind and rough sea stops her dead **D** and she pays off, out of control.

A luffing turn to pick up a mooring **E** also results in a dead stop. The full rudder and rapid change of direction robs her of forward way even before she comes head to wind.

Learning to judge how far a boat will carry her way is very difficult, but it is vital to know, whether under sail or engine.

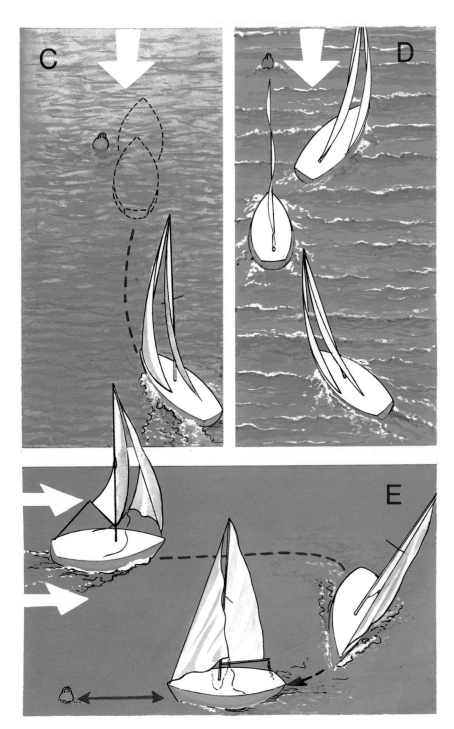

Shortening sail

A. Reefing while still sailing fast to windward is quite pointless when cruising. Slow her by easing sheets or by lying with helm a'lee and headsail eased, or, if making a headsail change, lie with the mainsail eased well off. The saying, 'the time to reef is when you first think about it' is a wise one and a reef put in early is usually a better reef than one done under stress. Reefing early when strong wind is imminent may leave the cruiser temporarily under canvased – the engine can be used to maintain speed, pending the arrival of the wind.

The smaller the area of sail carried, the more vital it is to ensure that the sails are well set. In bad weather resistance of hull and rigging increases so sails need maximum efficiency for windward work.

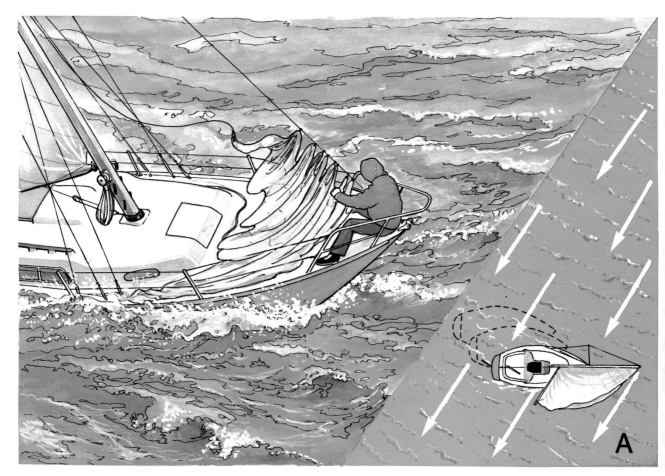

Reefing gear

B. Points reefing, used properly, results in a well setting sail. **C**. A variation of it is a laced reef or a system using elastic cord and a row of hooks along the boom. In both cases, pennants at tack and clew take the main loads and these are hauled down and secured first.

D. Roller reefing is simpler to use in the dark but does not guarantee a well setting sail. The gear may have a worm drive and handle (have a spare on board) or it may be of through-mast design, which is both simple and efficient. A drawback of roller reefing is that it makes the use of a kicking strap (vang) difficult.

The advent of mast reefing in which the luff of the sail rolls up inside the mast in similar fashion to roller headsail furling is further simplifying mainsail reefing.

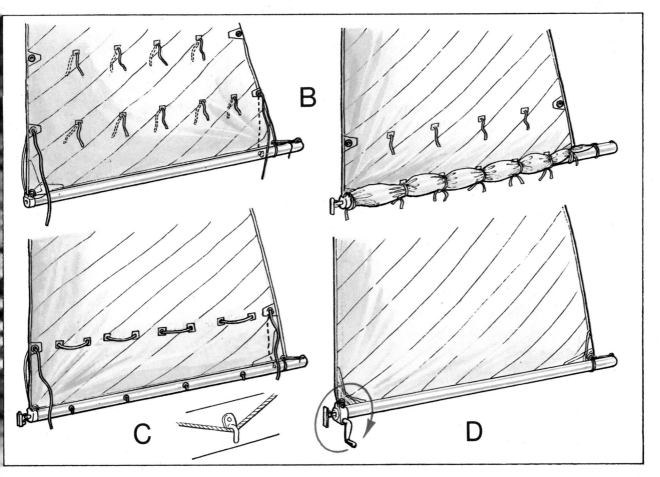

Improved reefing methods

A. Jiffy reefing has found favour over older methods. The cringle in the luff is pulled down to one of the hooks at the goose neck and the leech cringle is tightened down by means of a small block and tackle or winch on the boom. Even in small yachts some form of purchase must be used. Loose sail can be laced up or just bundled loosely for short periods.

B. To flatten the sail when roller reefing, try inserting spare battens or an empty sailbag as the sail is rolled down. This will tauten the foot of the sail and lessen the tendency for the shape to become fuller.

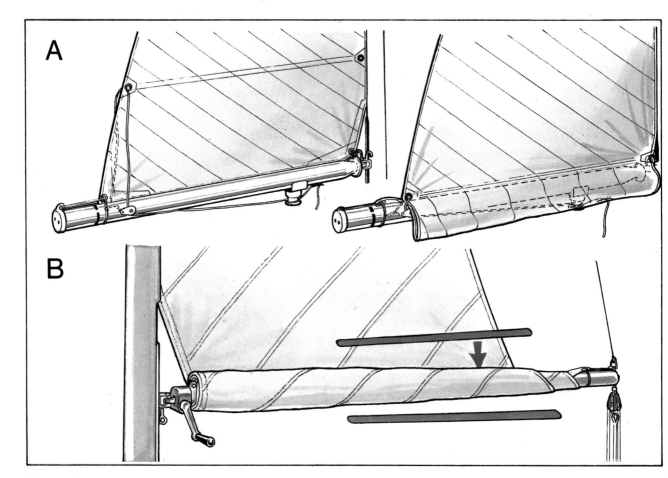

Sail shape
when reefed

C and **D** contrast the result of effective reefing with one which is badly organized. In **D** the loose luff of the jib and also the boom menacing the cockpit mean less performance just when it is needed in tight situations. **C**, reefed sails well set, are reassuring.

Reefing and shortening sail is often carried out under rough conditions or in the dark and it is essential that the job should be done properly, more especially if the boat has to be driven to windward. A boat with slack luffs, bad creases and wrinkles and loose,

baggy sails loses drive when she most needs it. Even if under motor the sails must be capable of being sheeted flat so that the boat can be pointed up close to the wind.

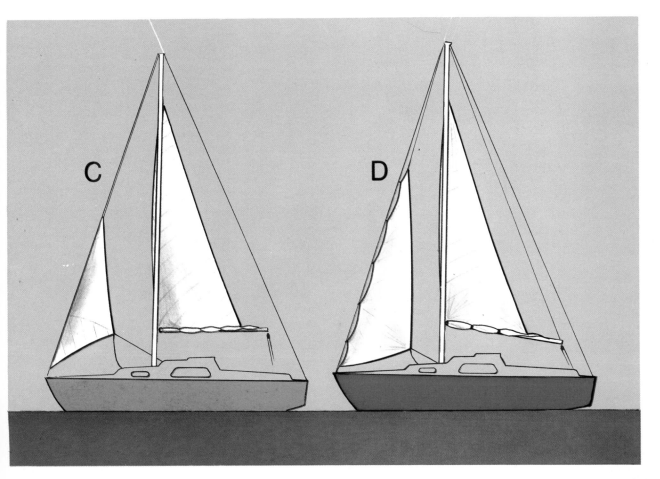

Changing a headsail

The first move in shortening a sail is usually the change down to a smaller headsail. As this frequently means the sea conditions have become rougher, the more forethought and system used, the easier and faster the job will be carried out. At **A1** the new sail in its bag is on deck and safely hitched to the cleat. (2) The sail is lowered, remembering to secure the halyard tail to the mast. (3) The halyard is detached from the sail and clipped to the pulpit. (4) The sheets are released from the clew.

B5. The old sail is bundled below and (6), the new sail hanked on, beginning with the tack but remembering, (7) to hitch its empty bag to a cleat to avoid loss.

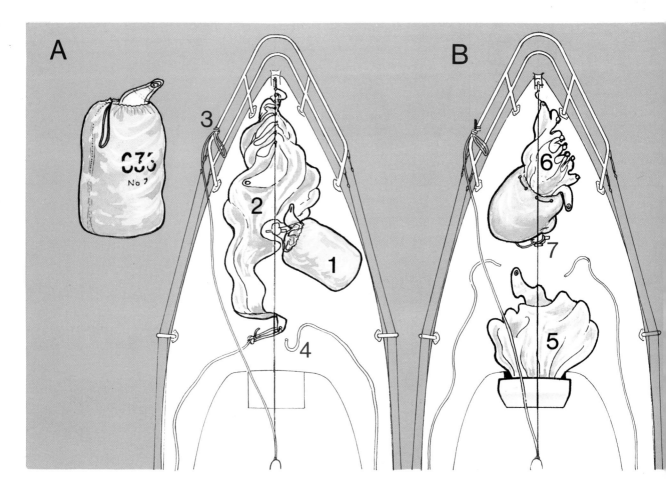

C. With the sail bag safely below, (8), and, (9–10), sheets and halyard attached, the sail can be hoisted.

D. It is sometimes better to hank on the new sail below the bottom hank of the existing sail. This means that the period during which the cruiser is sailing without a headsail set is much shorter. While this is usually of importance only when racing, there are times when a cruiser headsail change must also be carried out quickly and without losing sail power.

The change then consists of lowering the existing sail, unhanking it quickly to clear the forestay and, after changing the halyard, hoisting the new sail. At least one (leeward) sheet must be on the new sail. Subsequently the old sail is removed from the forestay and stowed.

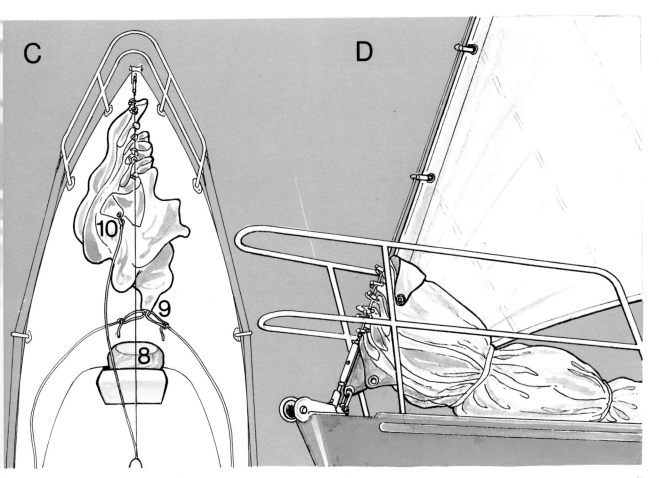

Roller headsails

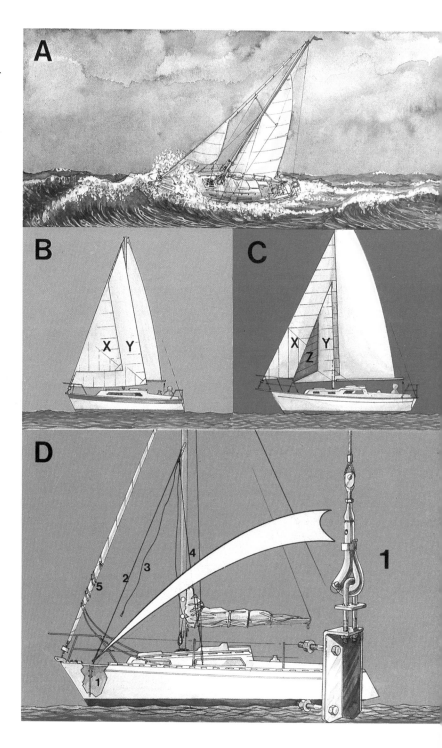

A. While there may be some loss of windward performance with a roller headsail, this is outweighed by easier handling and being able to carry the right sail area for wind conditions prevailing. However it is a mistake to suppose that it can be rolled small enough to serve as a storm jib for it then becomes shapeless and inefficient. A roller jib may cover winds ranging from calm to near-gale, but a storm jib is essential and a light ghoster an advantage.

B. Some roller systems permit sails to be changed easily. It must be remembered though that in a rising wind a half-rolled ghoster x-y must still be unrolled before it can be lowered and changed.

C. The cutter rig offers a compromise. The roller jib can be of moderate size X Rolling down to a force 5–6 area. Thereafter it is rolled away and the yacht sails on under her staysail Y until it is time to replace it with storm jib Z.

D. Single headsail rigs need provision for setting a separate storm jib such as a strong eye on deck braced to a bulkhead or pad below decks (1) plus a movable stay and spare halyard (2–3), which when not in use are stowed down the main shrouds (4). The stay is set up taut by means of a hook-on bottle screw or pelican hook (1 inset) and the jib is rolled up safely with several turns of the sheets around it, (5).

A stay provides a tighter luff and
easier handling. If the sail is to be set
'flying' it must first be 'stopped' (1)
unstretched, rolled and tied with easily
snapped twine which is parted by
sinching in on the sheet (2). When
lowering it the sail will flog dangerously (3) unless the yacht is run off
before the wind to shadow it behind
the mainsail.

As the sail unfurls by pulling the
sheet, a drum at the tack rolls up the
furling line. To roll the sail this line
is pulled thus rotating the drum. It is
essential that the line is kept taut
when unrolling or kinks may jam the
drum (1). When reducing sail the
sheets must also be kept taut or creases
may ruin the set of the half-rolled sail.

Should the drum jam and firm tension
applied by winch fail to free it the boat
may be left with too much sail for the
conditions and no means of either rolling or lowering the sail. Remove one
sheet and coil the other and have crew
pass it round and round (2) as the
boat is motored in tight circles (3),
with mainsail sheeted hard in or
lowered. Retaining one sheet is necessary otherwise when the sail is rolled
the clew would be out of reach.

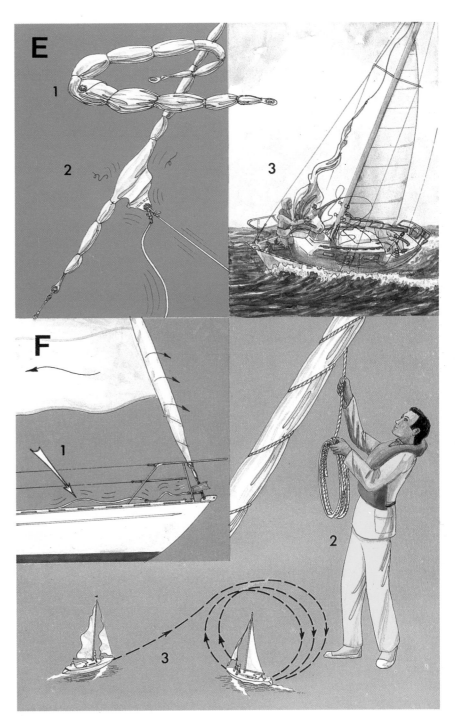

Man overboard
– Gear and what to do

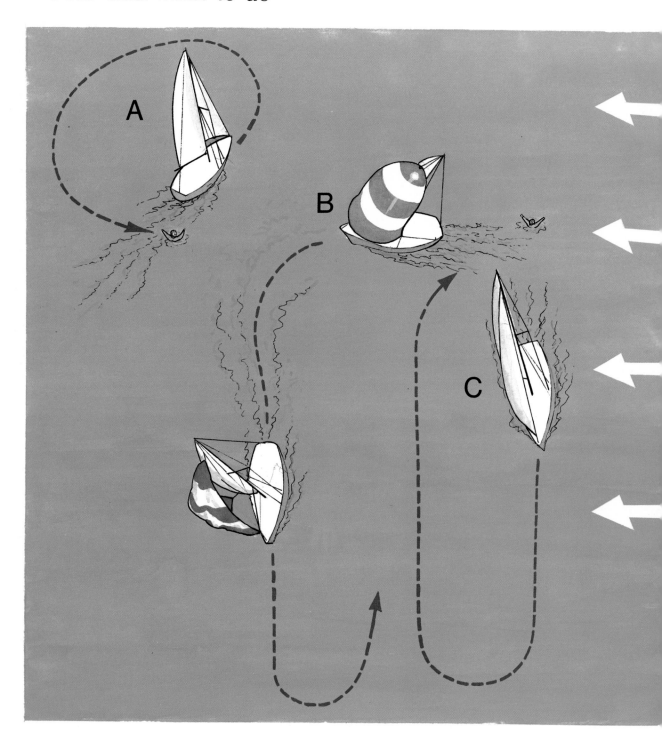

Coping with this emergency may call for great skill, self control and presence of mind. The more thought and planning given to it the greater the certainty of success. First considerations are the victim's ability to swim or to stay afloat – hence the importance of always wearing a lifejacket – and to keeping an eye constantly fixed upon the person in the water. Throw one lifebuoy immediately and then sail back close to him with a second lifebuoy available. Now there is time to think.

The boat must be stopped dead, right alongside him, which means that an approach must be made from downwind of him. At **A**, a gybe if made *at once* might bring the boat back to him head to wind. At **B**, under spinnaker, a reach off at 90 degrees gives time to hand the spinnaker and to return on a reciprocal heading and at **C**, a simple reaching return following a gybe to get downwind permits full control of speed. There are no classic manoeuvres which will guarantee success, only forethought and calmness can do that – *doing the right thing under existing circumstances.*

The temptation may be to lower all sail and start the engine and in some cases this may be right. A spinning propeller is a terrible danger to a man in the water though and once the man is alongside and secure, the engine must be *stopped*, not merely put into neutral, before attempting to haul him aboard anywhere near the after end of the boat.

Essential equipment

(1) Lifebuoy with a drogue or a 'skirt' to prevent it from drifting in the wind and out of reach.
(2) Self-operating light float attached to lifebuoy (also a whistle).
(3) Dan buoy flag marker.
(4) Floating throwing ring and line.
(5) Heaving line.
(6) Boarding ladder.

In the man overboard drill shown above the crew are experimenting with a lifting net which is lowered down the topsides to form a 'pocket' in which the casualty can be lifted aboard. Significant is the fact that the crew consists of four or more able bodied men. In real life a woman alone might have to cope.

Recovery

There are three major risks: losing sight of the man; delay and its consequences for a poor swimmer, especially in cold water; difficulty in hauling him back aboard. The latter can be a monstrous problem. The combined efforts of the man in the water and his rescuer(s) grow less with each unsuccessful attempt to pull him up and final exhaustion may overcome all – with fatal results. Panic exacts further toll of stamina. First, he must be reached and kept afloat.

At **A** a buoy has been thrown hastily and it is out of the man's reach. At **B** the cruiser is put about and passes close enough for a second buoy to be put into the man's hands. At **C**, she returns, under full control on a reach and with a boarding ladder ready in position. **D**. Lifelines should

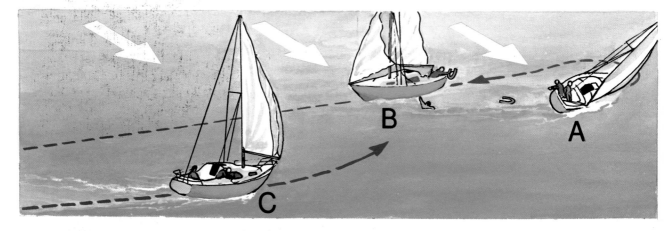

never be shackled to the after pulpit – a lashing can be cut, leaving a clear space for working. With a pair of wires only the lower need be cut. A rope bight or loop can be rigged with one end around a sheet winch. An active man can climb aboard on this, but not a weakened person – he should be secured with a bowline round the chest pending aid aboard.

A proper boarding ladder is the best aid of all but lacking one, a weakened swimmer can be pulled into a half-inflated dinghy **E**. (It can be carried permanently on deck in this state) from which hauling aboard is easy. Another method is to turn the man face outboard and lift with one man at each shoulder.

F. A method which has been known to work in real trouble, when the person is both heavy and weakened, is to drop the boom end into the cockpit and sheet it fast. The mainsail is then run completely out of its mast track and bundled overboard. By dragging the person into its slack and taking up on the halyard with each roll of the ship, he can be hauled up to deck level.

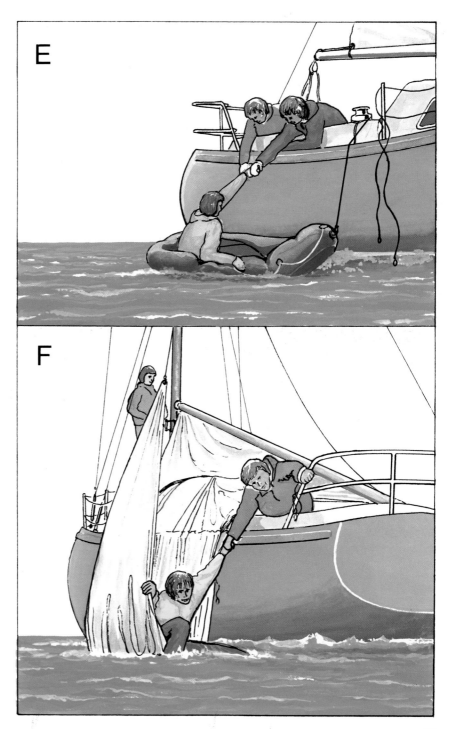

Knowing ropes

Use the right rope for the job and choose the best. Modern synthetics are hardwearing, long lasting – the better quality being treated to withstand sunlight, which can be injurious. Different types of rope are designed for various uses. **A**. 3-strand nylon has elasticity and is used for anchor lines and warps. Dacron© Terylene© has rather less elasticity. **B** is plaited with a straight laid core, a pliable rope for sheets. **C**. Double plait is softer and used for dinghy sheets. **D**. Cheaper synthetics can be used as floating rope, for mooring lines and rough uses. With these ropes knots tend to loosen themselves and are sometimes liable to parting if strained over a concentrated area. **E**, pre-stretched Dacron© used for halyards where elasticity is undesirable.

Basic knots, hitches and bends. **F**. Reef knot for joining ropes of similar thickness. **G**. Figure-of-eight knot for stopper knots in ends of jib sheets.

H. Clove hitch – a securing hitch. **J**. Rolling hitch used to secure to a rail, cable or stay when the pull is parallel and constant in direction. **K**. Fisherman's bend for securing to an anchor or similar purposes. **L**. The bowline, a non-slip bight.

All these knots, bends and hitches are prone to come undone when made in certain types of synthetic. Always leave plenty of spare ends and haul properly tight. It is important to be able to make these knots at top speed, also in the dark and to make them in ropes and lines of any thickness. Knowing which to use when, is a matter of practice. For instance, with heavy warps of equal thickness it would be safer to use two interlocking bowlines to join them rather than a reef knot. The knots shown here are a small selection of the many in regular use and every effort to learn the other common ones should be made.

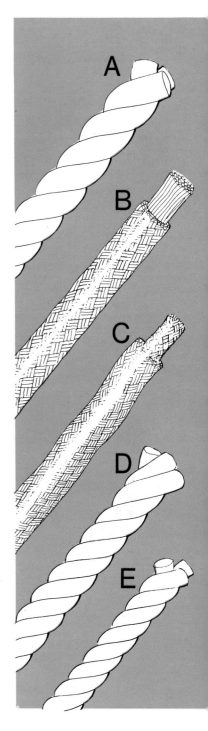

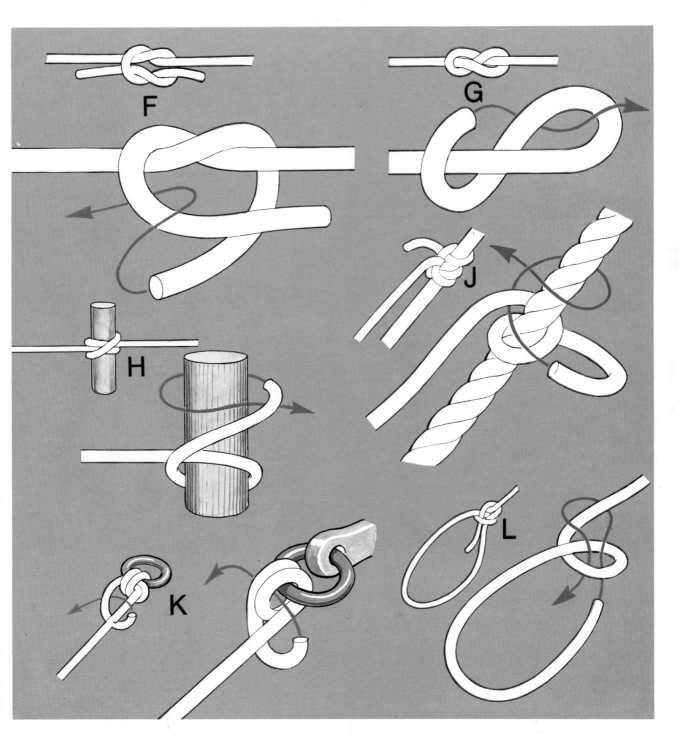

Securing with synthetics

A. An end tucked back through the lay will guard against this bowline coming undone. **B.** A seizing of small stuff on the ends is even more secure and it does not fractionally weaken the rope as it does in tucking through the lay, which disturbs the rope construction. **C.** This bowline on a post might lift itself off if the rope was stiff and springy, a complete round turn as shown makes it more secure. **D.** The tugboat hitch, used when securing to a post, for example when making up an anchor warp or chain, never pulls itself so tight that it cannot be undone easily, as in the case of certain other hitches. The bight of the slack end is taken under, up and over as shown several times. It cannot come undone.

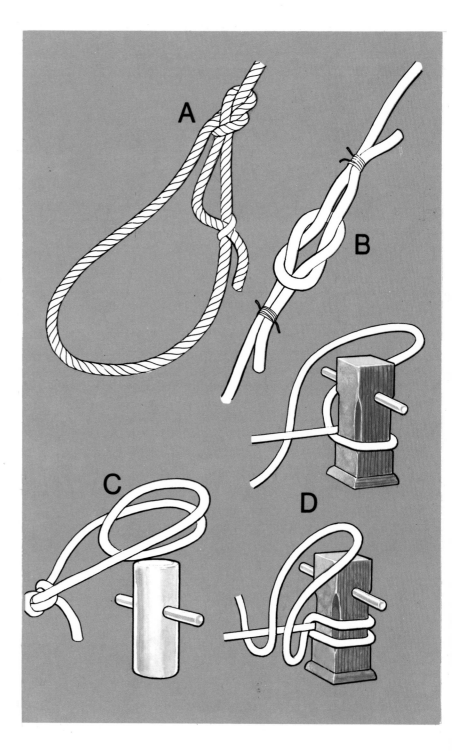

Coiling

E. Most ropes are laid (twisted) right-handed or clockwise and they must be coiled clockwise. The coils are laid from one hand to the other, shaking out any twists before each coil is handed. The exception is certain double plaited ropes which are not coiled but allowed to form natural figure of eight loops.

F. A buntline hitch is the correct way to make up a coil so that it can be used later. Pass the bight over the head of the coil.

G. Stopping a coiled warp is essential if it is to be readily usable in a hurry. Use yarns pulled from odd short lengths of rope or else use breaking stuff, easily snapped.

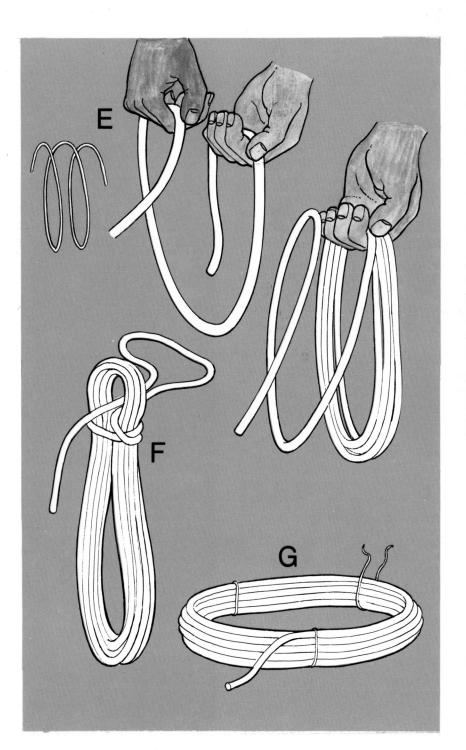

Halyards

Never make a halyard fast with only a couple of figure of eight turns or it will pull tight and may jam. **A**. Use a full round turn followed by two or more figure of eight turns. **B**. Jam the slack end hard down in the top of the cleat between halyard and cleat.

The coil can then be hung as shown in **C** and **D** by pulling a loop (bight) through the coil and settling it over the top horn of the cleat. If the bight is first taken behind (between standing halyard and mast) and then settled over the horn, it will be more secure.

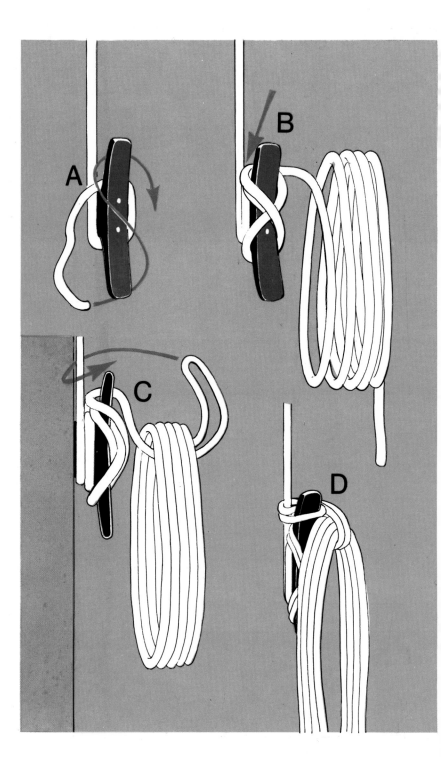

Planning a
cruise

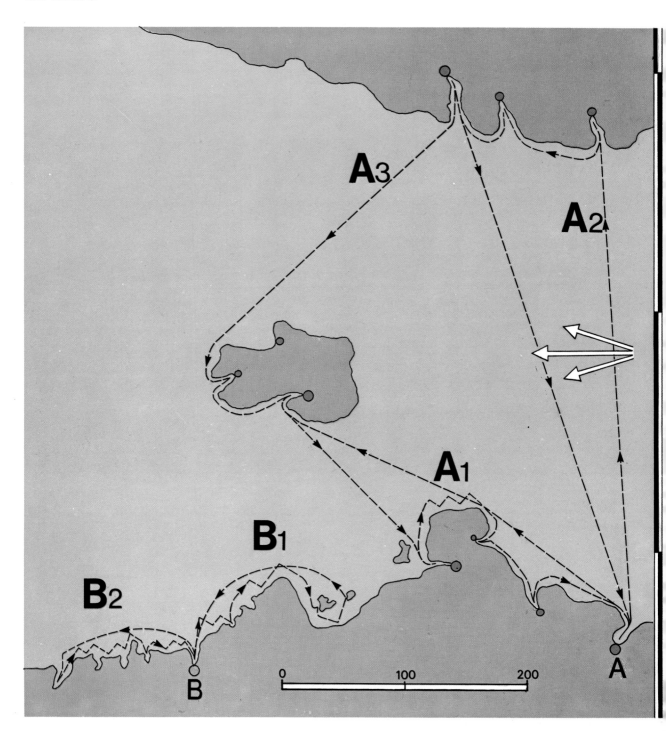

A₃

A₂

A₁

B₁

B₂

B

A

0   100   200

easurable cruising under sail is not ependent upon distance covered in given time. One must find the ght 'pace' for each particular boat nd crew. One can have more fun ithin a few miles of home than any have in covering vast distances.

ow far – in how long?

he imaginary cruising ground hown here offers a choice of disnces. Note the prevailing wind ith length of arrow indicating kelihood of direction. Port **A** is a oor area with lee shores preominating. From it, however, two reas can be visited on a cruise; **A1** tals a round mileage of 520 or cruise **2** 560 nautical miles. **A3**, 640 miles

covers both areas. All give reaching or running courses with close fetches home. **A1** has a final short beat.

Port **B** offers shorter distances in coastal hops, **B1** with short daily beats and a long run home, total mileage 210 and **B2** gives a long run to begin with and short windward hops home, total 200 nautical miles.

Plainly, boats based at port **B** can also make longer cruises to the island or the distant shores but crew strength and time available, in that order, must be the deciding factors. Bad weather could hold a yacht weatherbound in port or force the gamble of a wild dash for home at the expiration of a holiday.

Cruising is pleasure and leisure. It should not be made a matter of time keeping and running to schedule – that belongs to life ashore.

Cruising in company and enjoying the fun of getting together at the end of a passage is both very enjoyable and helpful should one or more of the owners happen to be learners. In the picture above the weather is calm and sharing one mooring (provided it is known to be big enough) is safe enough for a short stay. In fresher conditions three of these yachts would be lying to their own anchors.

The passage plan

A passage plan is not a series of courses to be followed rigidly, it simply represents forward thinking which familiarises the navigator with the problems. It examines options, charts, pilot information, tidal patterns, dangers and ports of refuge. Working to a plan ensures that nothing is forgotten.

Changed circumstances of wind and weather may mean abandoning the plan soon after starting, but the navigator is now familiar with chart, distances and tidal patterns and alternative plans will have been reviewed.

Usually there are critical arrival times to be considered, e.g. a daylight arrival if the port is not lit, state of tide on arrival and tidal gates at headlands. The total distance to be covered and the average speed expected in the light of a weather forecast thus dictates departure time. For this reason it is best to make the plan as close to sailing day as possible. Plans made well in advance are still useful but less realistic.

In most cases arrivals are later than planned because estimated speeds are usually too optimistic, this can also lead to excessive motoring which detracts from the pleasure of sailing. A modest 3–4 knots is a typical average under sail for small cruisers.

The plan should include: charts, pilotbooks, almanac, tidal atlases, times of high water at standard ports relating to tidal information, critical times at headlands etc, principal buoyage, lights and radio beacons plus characteristics of value on passage, dangers, ports of refuge details, courses, distances and latest met. information plus probabilities.

An example of a passage plan. Course **1** is 50 n miles from **D** to **C**. The headland **A** is a tide-gate and the destination, river **C** has a bar and can only be entered during daylight and between one hour before and one hour after HW. Thus the plan must allow a fair tide for passing the headland and an arrival at the destination around HW. The wind is expected to be moderate in strength but the yacht will be close-hauled plus some short beats.

Course **2** is almost ten n miles longer with more tacking and need for daylight when passing the narrows at **B**. The first leg however, is less close-hauled and will be faster, although a fair tide will be needed for the final beat.

Choosing course **1**. The tidal stream at **A** is fair between 0800 and 1400 and HW at destination **C** is 0600 and 1845. With this wind there will be a nasty tide race during the strongest hours of fair tide at headland **A**.

Option: Reach headland **A** on the last of the fair stream at 1300 leaving only 6 plus hours to reach destination **C** at the latest time for crossing the bar (1945). At a 3 knot average this might take 8 hours and at 4 knots 6 hou A gamble and much hard motoring

Option: Reach headland **A** on t first of the fair stream soon after 08 leaving plenty of time to reach t destination. This would mean saili from port **D** at around 2300 the pr vious night assuming an average knots or 0100 assuming 4 knots.

Option: A night passage since hea land **A** and point **X** have lighthous Leaving **D** at 1100 we might pass t headland around 2000 and arrive **C** about 0530, assuming an average 3 knots.

On course **2** we need to arrive at cha nel **B** at much the same time as catching the first of the fair stream Headland **A**, thus being sure of a fa stream during the 20 mile beat th follows. We also have to ensure th we tackle channel **B** in daylight. Wi the wind freer on the first leg we ca bank on averaging 4 knots (may more) and departing from **D** at 23 should bring us to the channel **B** 0800. The only snag now is that v have a whole day in which to beat t last 20 miles. We may have to heav to off the river bar and wait sor hours.

A dominant shift of wind direction strength could alter the whole pl and the change might come while the middle of it. It is when the mi and body are tired that the real val of having thought things through comfort and in advance becom apparent.

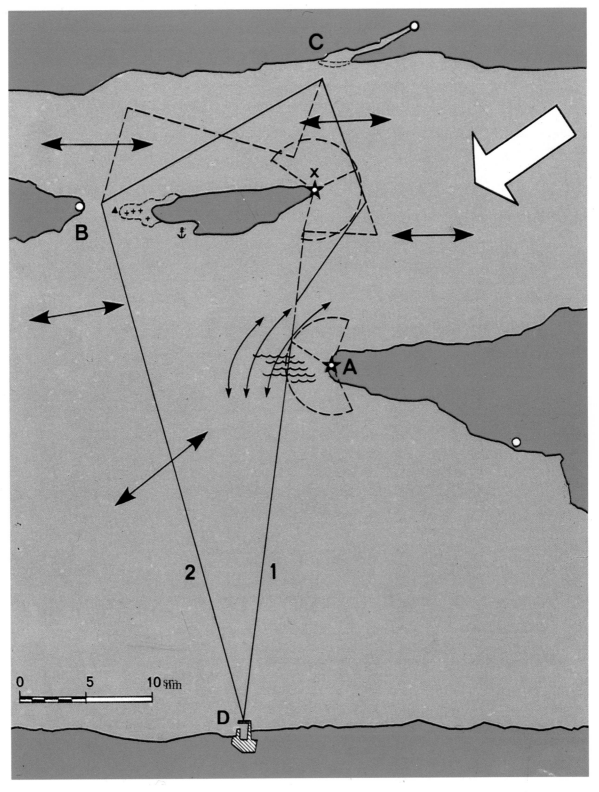

77

Passage making preparations

A sound suitable cruiser, with the necessary stores for living, repairing and navigating must be assumed. Charts, pilot books, an almanac, tables, instruments and chart table equipment must be up to date and functional. The skipper should have mastered basic navigation.

The basic essentials are steering compass, log and hand lead or echo-sounder. These instruments are only as valuable as they are accurate and, if accurate, they are only as valuable as the skill of their user. A chart which has not been corrected up to date is a potential danger.

Likewise too few charts. Have large scale harbour or river charts, also detailed coastal charts and save the small scale charts for open sea passage making.

Follow meteorological reports consecutively and begin listening to them two days prior to departure so that the weather trends can be appreciated.

. Make regular checks on compass
ad log. A simple check of steering
ompass is to take bearings on mast
ad backstay in line, from an in-
atable (therefore non-magnetic)
nghy towed astern while motoring
a steady heading. Take each
ain heading in turn (N, NE, E etc)
ad note the difference between the
nghy hand-bearing compass and
e ship's steering compass.

rst check the hand bearing compass
hore against known chart bearings.
bucket towed from the dinghy stern
ay be needed to hold her straight.

he log can be checked against that
a fellow yachtsman or whenever a
urrent free' opportunity to run be-
veen fixed sea marks can be taken.

. Some coasts have measured disnces (x) shown on charts, used for
ecking ship's speed against log.
lake timed runs at slack tide, or if
ere is a tidal current, take the
verage of several runs.

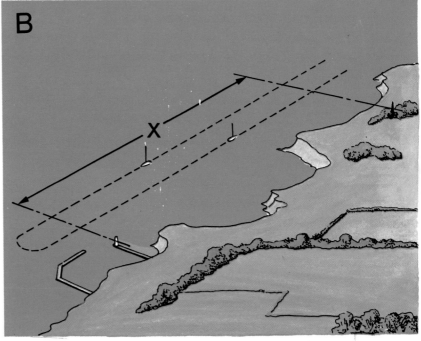

Tidal strategy

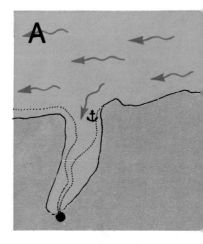

In waters beset by tidal streams a small sailing craft must 'work' her fair tides, particularly if her course lies to windward when she is coasting.

Our skipper has a leg of 45 miles to windward before him and he knows that he must use the full 6 hours (approximately) of fair tide to best advantage. Thus he may count upon (let's say) an 8-mile lift, leaving 37 miles to be made good.

At **A**, he drops down river the previous evening and anchors at the mouth, where he waits for the foul tide outside to ease. At **B**, he gets under way and with one hour of weak foul tide still to run he gets well to sea. This means that he will be in the best position to take full advantage of the tidal stream when it begins to run fair. With 37 miles to

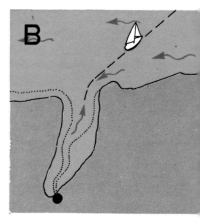

sail (two long tacks) he must average over 5 knots if he is to arrive before the tidal stream turns foul. If he cannot do this under sail, he may use engine power to maintain his average, or he may begin working closer inshore as soon as the foul stream sets in. There he may find slacker currents. He would of course need to be an efficient chart reader or to have local knowledge to do so in safety. At **C**, the arrows show how the tide is turning foul at the headland while still running fair close inshore.

In calm weather, an alternative is to kedge out the foul tide, lying to a kedge anchor for about 4 hours during the strongest period of the foul run. When kedging a tide, either at sea or in temporary shelter inshore, the ship is regarded as being still under way and a proper watch must be maintained.

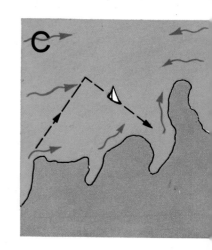

The weather

In some latitudes the weather follows predictable seasonal patterns, in others it varies continually. There are also regions where summer calms prevail punctuated by violent winds peculiar to the climate and the area, such as the 'Southerly Buster' of the Antipodes or the Mistral of the western Mediterranean. The cruising man must know his climate and know what to expect.

In areas where high and low pressure systems follow in succession, fine and rough weather alternate. The 'story' must be studied for a few days before sailing. In this way a skipper begins his cruise with a knowledge of the developing pattern and the subsequent weather forecasts make much more sense to him.

In the very simplified weather map shown here, the numbers represent a period of five days. In (1), depression **Y** is passing, with decreasing wind and clearing sky. By the next day, (2), a ridge of high pressure is approaching which continues into the following day, (3), with sunny seas and calm sailing. The unwary, who is not watching his weather could be tricked into embarking on a long passage but days (4–5) see the arrival of depression **X** and a resumption of windy weather.

A wise skipper would realize that the improving weather was merely a pressure ridge between two lows. He would either advance his plans in order to make his passage while it lasted, or he would be prepared to hole up in shelter until the second low had gone through.

Not only wind strength and sea state will be affected but wind direction also and the shifting winds will be a major influence on his passage plans. In areas where summer calms prevail, he may have to make his sailing passages according to the onshore–offshore thermal winds of daytime and early night – or he fuels up in preparation for long passages under power.

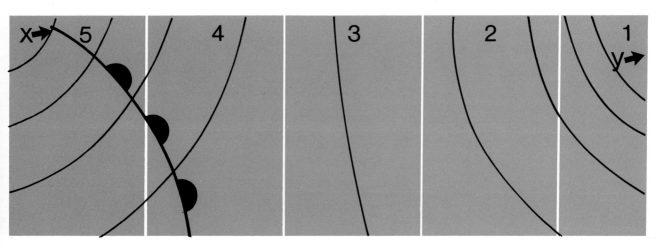

Final approach

If the destination is unfamiliar and the passage has been long and tiring, extra care is needed in the final approach. Our cruising yacht may be at (a) or (b) and it is night. From (a) the loom of the town lights is visible over the hill, also two of the navigational lights. From (b) however a mass of town lights can be seen also. There may be a temptation to head straight for them.

The navigator must identify the navigational lights and then single out those which are the crucial ones for a safe approach. In this case a pair of leading or range lights must be brought into line from a position well outside the bay.

If pilot books and charts are studied in advance, the navigator will know what to look for. However, if anything puzzles him or doesn't seem quite right, the final run in must not be tackled until the mystery has been solved.

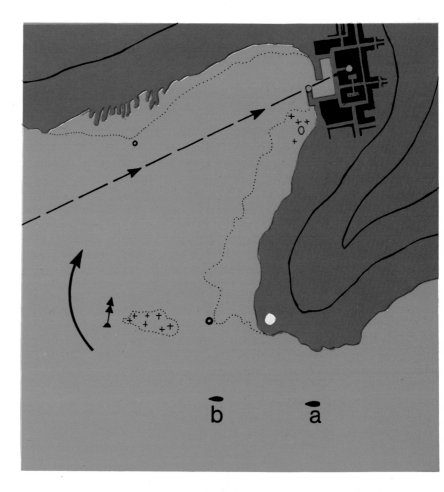

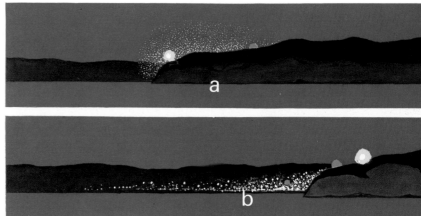

Harbour lights

Unless there are leading or range lights to provide a safe approach, careful identification of harbour entrance lights is needed, also a minute examination of the chart for any inconspicuous dangers – perhaps marked by an unlit buoy or beacon pole.

Quite often harbour entrance lights to small ports are fixed red and green. They may also be weak by comparison to other red and green lights in the town, such as garage, casino or advertising neon signs.

From well out to sea it is all too easy to head for the wrong light. Always approach from a fixed position thereby knowing what the *correct* light should bear from where you are. If you cannot fix your position accurately, proceed with extreme care, checking depth soundings against the chart. Decide from the chart where the dangers lie and shape your approach to avoid those areas until such time as you have sorted out the correct light.

Errors in pilotage

Basic pilotage, simple and safe, is essential knowledge for all seagoers but unsuspected errors can creep in which can be dangerous. By anticipating them, by recognizing them, they can be dealt with in time.

A steering or plotting error of only 1 degree represents a 1-mile off course error in a distance of 60 miles **A** and errors of 3 and more degrees are far more common. At **B** the port to port navigator sees two headlands when he makes his landfall. Not knowing his error, which should he head for? He might head confidently for where he supposed the port to lie, while heading for an unsafe stretch of coast. **C**. By making an appraisal of all possible errors to course (steering, compass error, tidal set, log error, leeway etc) he ends up with a 'box' within which his true position must lie **B**. Imprecise navigation perhaps, but he can now make a safer decision in his approach.

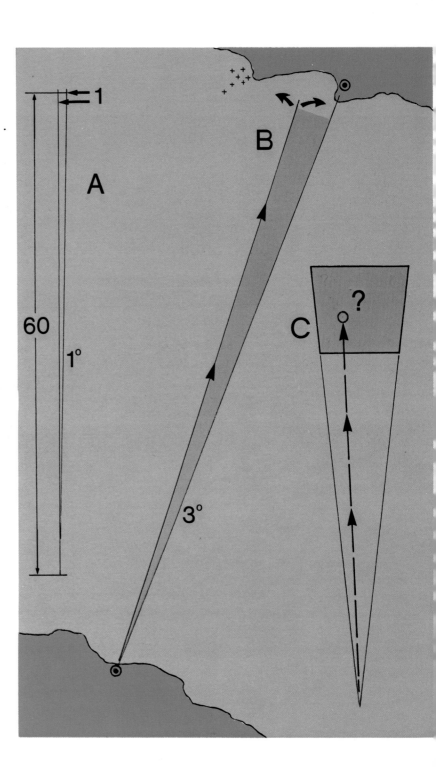

Drift and leeway

In rough weather the surface of the sea drifts to leeward but light displacement, shoal draft craft are affected by it far more than deeper, heavier boats with their lower immersion in more solid water. **D** will drift faster than **E**.

Side-slip while sailing or leeway also varies between boats and it varies too according to the angle of sailing and the state of the sea. Cruiser **F** is making 5 degrees of leeway in smooth conditions but at **G** with a rough sea meeting her starboard bow she may make a great deal more. A navigator must never assume that the leeway allowance made for one course will be suitable for all courses.

Leeway can be estimated by taking a bearing of the wake astern and checking it against the heading actually being steered.

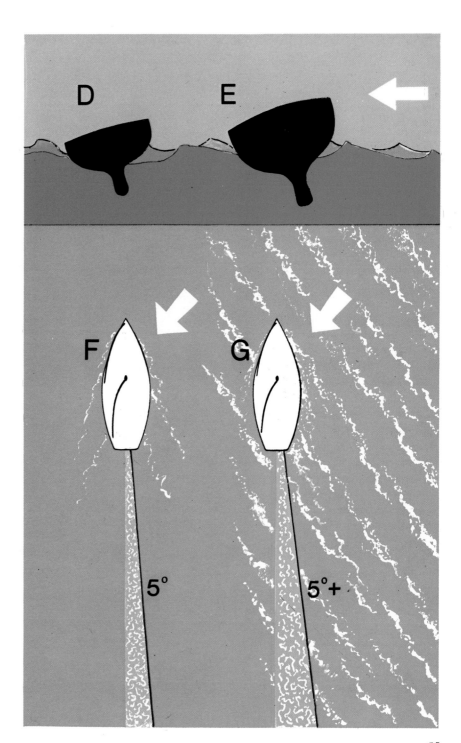

Helmsman's error

Concentration on the steering compass alone tires a helmsman and can result in an erratic course made good. He should divide his gaze between compass, bows and horizon – the stars at night. This means that he subconsciously corrects the swing of the ship relative to the view ahead and, **A**, needs only an occasional glance at the compass as a check.

On the dead run **B**, a helmsman subconsciously plays safe to avoid a gybe and tends to steer to windward. The use of boom guy or vang to hold the boom forward results in more peace of mind and usually a better course steered. In rough conditions with an inexperienced man at the helm, it is better to order a course which he can steer, and keep to, rather than one he cannot hold. Closehauled, in a squally wind, the helmsman at **C** may have a tendency to luff, resulting in an error to windward. A broad reaching course in a cruiser **D** which carries heavy weather-helm will also produce an error to windward of the course plotted.

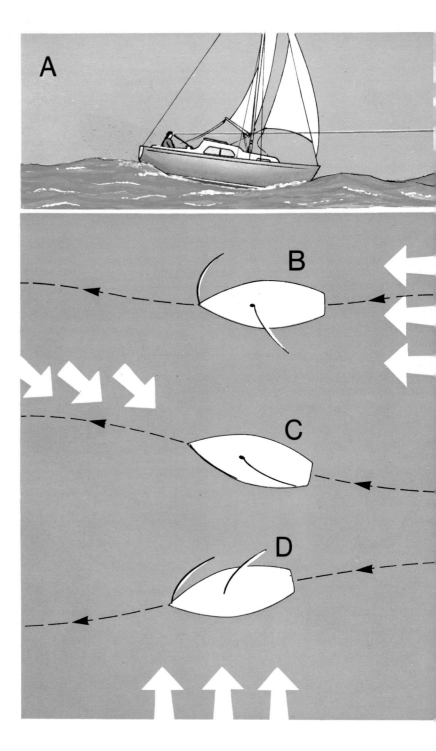

Log errors

E. a long over-reading total distance run may be due to the steering of an erratic course by a series of poor or careless helmsmen. A log may under-read in drifting weather, when the cruiser is moving very slowly, **F**. This is often more noticeable in the case of a towed log rotator. **G**. Running in a steep, following sea may cause over-reading, but much depends upon the instrument and how efficiently it is installed. A towed rotator log suffers worst in these conditions, but other types, including electronic logs, are capable of over-reading. Ideally, any through-hull impellers because there is constant variation in pressure on either side of the keel. Check at the start of each season. It is better to have a small *known* error than to assume accuracy.

Accurate knowledge of distance run, when approaching the coast in bad weather and low visibility is vital. Radio bearings or echo sounder readings cannot always be trusted to tally with the chart.

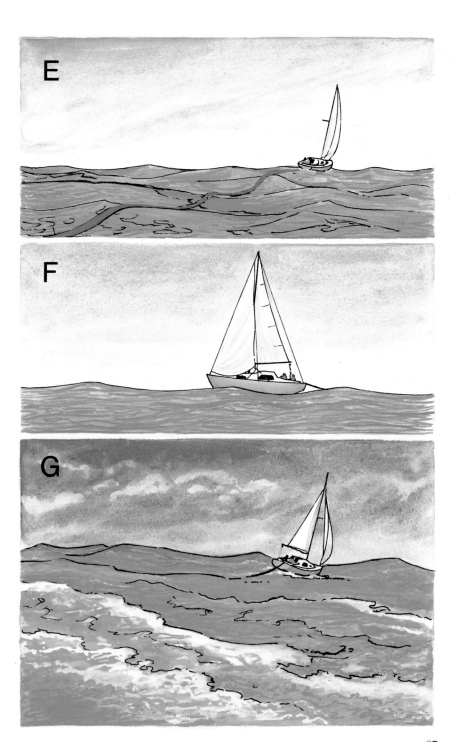

Anticipation

A long awaited light appearing suddenly, just where it should be, encourages the navigator to believe that he is sailing course **B** and seeing buoy (y). He may even see lights on shore which tally with the expected haven lights and he alters course towards them.

In fact, he was on course **A**, heading for buoy (x) and the 'haven' lights were pure coincidence. Unless he is very lucky he may be wrecked.

Always identify a light positively b its type and light characteristic firs even if you believe that it is the on you want. Then check the chart t find a corresponding description. B especially vigilant when you ar tired. Hallucination concernin lights at sea is a common pitfall fc tired seamen.

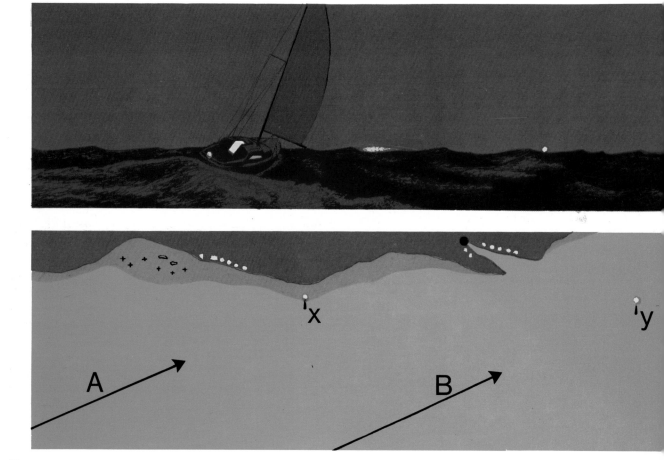

Horizon errors

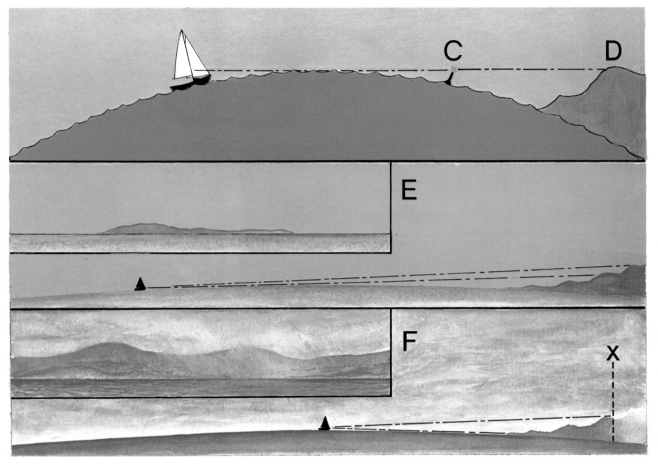

From eye level in a small cruiser the horizon may only be about 3.5 miles away. Thus, objects beyond this distance will be partly or wholly hidden from view. The buoy **C** 'dips' up into view and at night its light may be hidden intermittently by wave tops, causing a false light sequence to be seen. Check distant buoy sequences several times. The best aid is a stopwatch. Check beyond any doubt the time sequence and *then* consult the chart. This averts the risk of making the light fit the chart or wishful thinking. Note that the mountain peak **D** would be the only part of it visible by day.

At extreme range, a coast might appear as in **E**, the foreground hidden by the horizon. In poor visibility extending only to **X**, the same coast, **F**, looks quite different as it is the foreground cliffs which hide the high land beyond. Thus a coastal outline can vary between a series of sharp, distant peaks and a grey wall – even a sudden view of a line of surf!

False headlands

Headlands dominate most coastal passages: faster currents, rougher water and offlying rocks make many of them miniature Cape Horns. They can also deceive.

A. The cruiser, closing with the land at (1) may mistakenly think himself to be at (2) and in safe water, the coastal bulge looking from inshore like a headland. If he moves seaward to (2) however, the real headland comes into view beyond.

At **B**, **C** and **D** another headland has three different faces according to the position of the viewer. A navigator may have a preconceived idea of the appearance of a headland from an earlier visit. He may approach it a second time from a new angle and not recognize it – or mistake some other headland because it looks familiar.

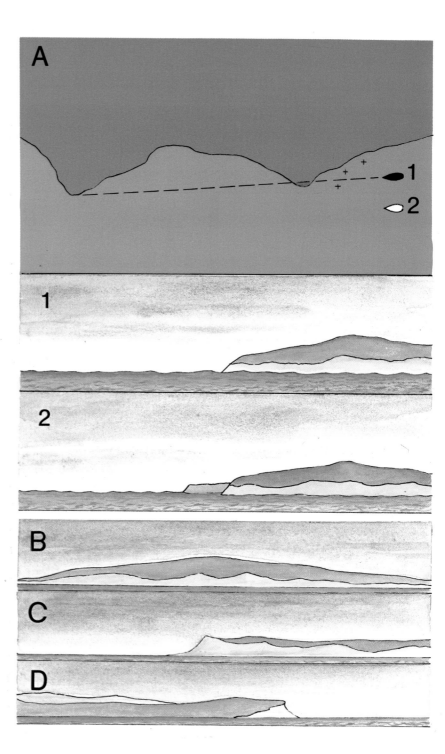

A fast run into ever-narrowing waters when headlands must be identified correctly beyond any doubt—not always an easy matter when the navigator is also needed on the helm. Pilotage by eye calls for continuous and undistracted concentration.

Angles can deceive

E. The cruiser is leaving harbour. The navigator knows that the buoy outside the harbour, which he must make for, lies straight to seaward from the harbour entrance and so he fails to plot a course to steer.

He has been berthed in basin (a), therefore his course from basin towards the entrance is an oblique one, but he *feels* as if he were going straight out, as if from (b). He sees the nearer buoy, guarding the shoal, and makes for it, leaving it to port in the belief that it is the more distant fairway buoy. He runs aground. Always check by the compass heading. Never make casual assumptions.

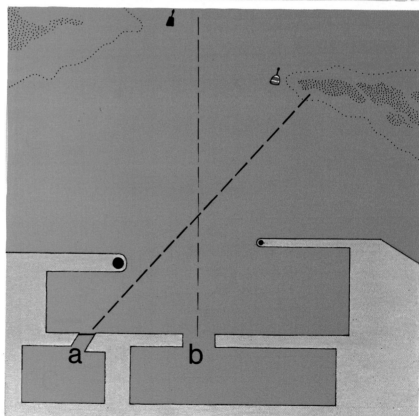

False headings again

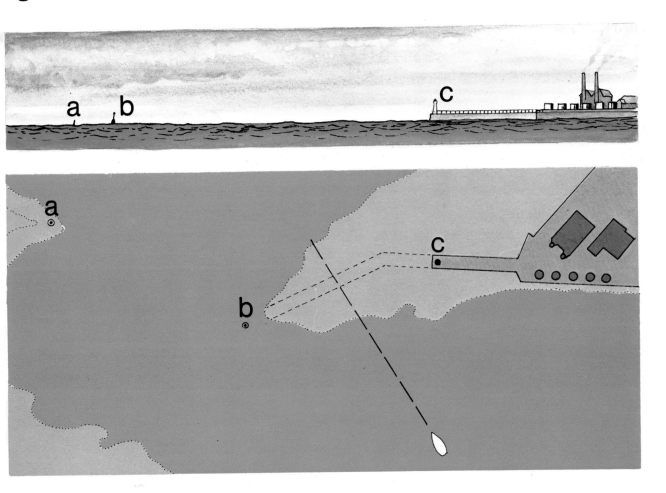

Pilotage by eye calls for a keen sense of direction, position and orientation. It is an art which is only slowly learned for some and a natural gift for others.

In the situation below there are three beacons, (a) on a distant shoal, (b) outside a submerged breakwater and (c) on the visible breakwater. The navigator sees the view at top left, but fails to take account of the distant beacon (a), assuming carelessly that (b) is the distant rock. He rounds the breakwater, crossing the dangerous submerged part – or attempting to do so.

Often, what appears to be obvious is actually a snare for the unwary. Close chart study and an ability to identify the features shown on the chart with the features seen and the angle of the ship's course relative to the lie of the land, are the secret of safe pilotage. When there are currents to contend with it can become risky to rely upon the eye alone.

False headings again

The cruiser is being steered by eye on a course to leave the light-vessel close to starboard. No compass course has been set. In the diagram it can be seen that there is a strong tidal current setting on the port side and there are shoal waters to starboard. Being under engine in a calm, there is no wind direction to aid the helmsman's sense of direction. Although he maintains a heading that keeps the lightship on his starboard bow, the current is setting him fast to starboard, (a) then (b) then (c) and it is only a matter of time before the cruiser will be in shallow waters.

Sheering across a track can happen when heading almost directly into the current. The only safe means of discovering the error is to keep an eye on the steering compass heading.

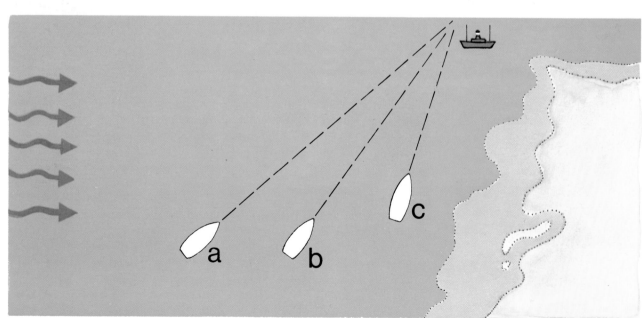

False fixes

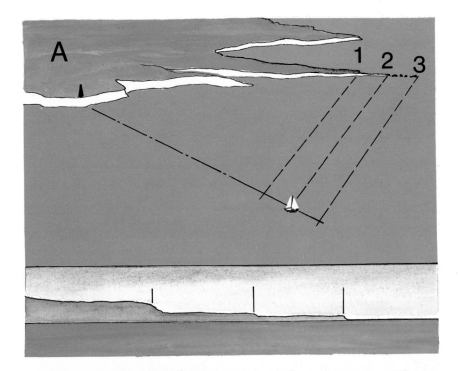

Compass bearings should only be taken on definite and identifiable objects, plainly shown on the chart. At **A** one bearing is reliable but the other, a headland, is not. Depending upon the state of the tidal height and visibility the extreme tip of the headland might appear as (1), (2) or (3). Whenever possible three suitably spaced objects should be chosen.

B The sighted objects chosen produce an angle that is too narrow to provide an accurate cross. The slightest compass inaccuracy or rough water could produce a wide area of error. Objects should be as near 90 degrees as possible and this angle be bisected by the bearing from a third object, if one can be found. In **C** the area of possible error is far smaller.

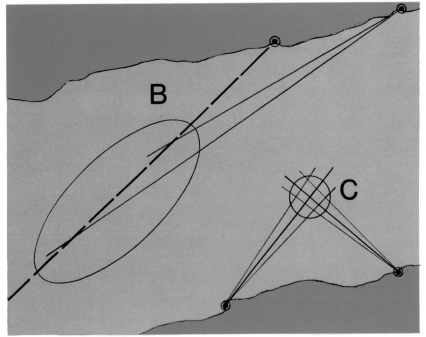

False soundings

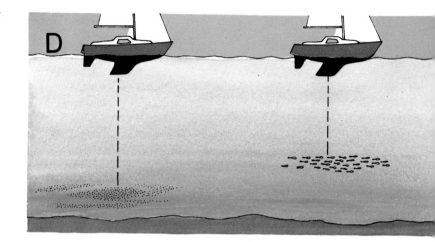

D Layers of suspended silt or large shoals of fish can give a false echo-sounder reading. Errors due to use are more common such as the situation **E**. The yacht on her starboard tack encounters a more gently shelving river bed (1) as she approaches the bank than she does when on her port tack, where the steep-to bed results in an instant fall in echo-sounder reading. With so little warning she could run aground at (2). The following starboard tack takes her to (3), the 'sounder still showing deep water because she has run into a gully. When she tacks she will run aground.

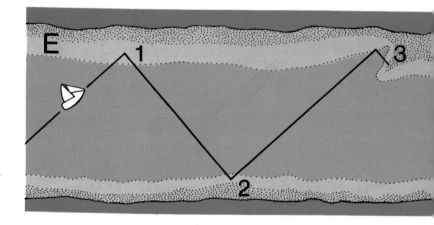

In **F**, a landfall in fog, echo-sounder readings related to chart soundings could lead the navigator at (5) into thinking himself to be approaching the river at (4).

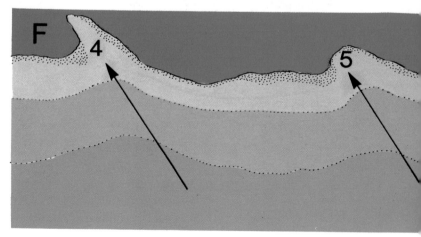

Shoal water mooring. The tranquility of such a mooring is generous compensation for the inconvenience of dragging a dinghy tender down some muddy foreshore, far from the amenities of a busy marina. It is a different dimension of sailing, fortunately not sought by the majority of owners.

Deceptive chart scale

A. On a small scale chart a group of buoys may appear to be very close together, unless the scale is examined carefully. A navigator, rounding the bank which is guarded by three buoys might expect from a casual glance at his chart, to be able to see all three at the same time. In fact he might only see the nearest buoy, the others being mere pin pricks (lower view). Always try in advance to form a clear idea of what you can expect to see.

In buoy spotting it is also unwise to stare fixedly at where you *think* the buoy should be. Search the horizon systematically, even in directions where it might seem to be impossible to find a buoy. Course angle and minor pilotage errors play tricks on you and your buoy could be far to seaward where you'd least expect it.

Deceptive buoyage

B. This tacking yacht is unable to steer a direct course along the curving channel and this is confusing to her navigator's sense of direction. He should tack and put in a short leg (a) which permits him to tack again and sail up the channel. Instead, he sees the buoys aligned as in the lower view and stands on, ultimately cutting a corner into shallow water, (b).

The only safeguard when running a buoyed channel is to identify each and every buoy before approaching it and check it against the chart and against ship's *heading*. Unless a compass course is noted it is quite possible for a helmsman on the wind to luff for a wind shift and bring a (for example) port hand buoy over to his starboard bow – fooling the navigator who is conning by eye alone.

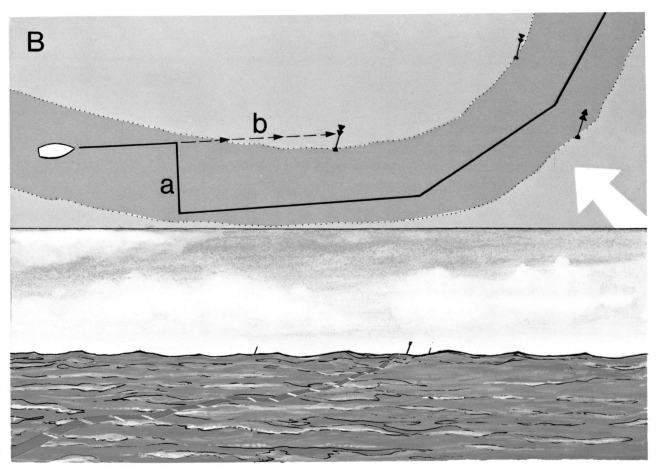

Coasting complications
– Apparent wind

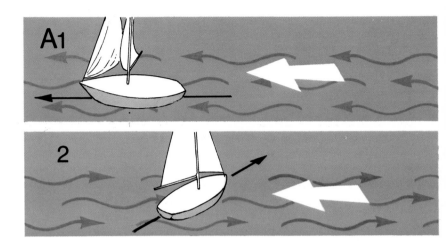

True wind is that which is experienced while stationary, apparent wind is what happens to the true wind when a boat begins to move. At **A1** the 2-knot wind becomes an *apparent* calm when the running yacht is carried downwind on a 2-knot current. Conversely, **A2** if the 2-knot current was carrying her against the 2-knot wind and she was sailing closehauled at 2-knots, the total apparent wind felt would be, roughly, 6 knots.

At **B** a closehauled cruiser sailing at 6 knots, helped by a 4-knot current and facing a 24-knot wind experiences a gale force wind of 34 knots. Had she been running, with the current fair **C**, her crew would have felt only a moderate breeze of 14 knots. With strong currents and fresh breezes be prepared for very rough conditions when forces oppose.

Beating seaward at slack water and in
a light breeze, this small cruiser makes
a delightful picture. In the narrow
entrance to the river though, her crew
may meet with some sudden shifts in
wind direction and strength as the
wind funnels and eddies. Reading the
shape of the land and anticipating the
wind changes is part of the sailing art.

Coasting complications
– Wind bend

Generally, the wind blowing along a coastline will 'bend' at the edge of the coast. (1), is the true wind and (2) is the wind bend crossing the coast. At (3) however, the wind is funnelling strongly down the valley, while at (4) there is an area of wind 'shadow' or calm under the lee of the cliff.

Where different air streams converge there may be eddies and a cruiser may encounter baffling shifts and violent squalls interspersed with short calms. Watch the water for signs of squalls but near high cliffs remember that they can strike downwards without such warnings. Watch other yachts, smoke, trees ashore and so on. Don't be caught unawares.

Judging distance off

A. Coasting either too close or too far offshore affects one's ability to identify coastal features. At view (1) the observer is too close for an overall view, at view (2), four miles off, details of headlands and the general trend of the land can be seen while at view (3), ten miles, headlands are hard to distinguish and inland hills dominate.

B. Surf breaking on a beach gives a rough guide to distance. With an average eye height of eight feet the sea horizon is 3.25 miles away, if visible; distance is this or less. If just hidden it is 3.25 miles plus.

C. A headland may have an unmarked offlying danger. On the chart, measure a short distance inland from the point (tower, church etc) and use this as a 'unit', then check the number of units offshore to clear the danger, in this case four. Sighting with the dividers at arm's length, first measure off the same unit on the actual tower and then open the dividers to unit X_4 and sight offshore from the headland. The line of sight must be roughly at right angles, otherwise measurements become foreshortened and unreliable.

D. Doubling the angle. When a shore mark bears 45 degrees from the bow, note the log reading and note again when the object bears 90 degrees; distance travelled in tideless conditions **X** equals distance off **Y**. A fair tide results in a closer (therefore safer) estimate. It is useful to tape the guardrails at 45 and 90 degree positions on port and starboard for sighting purposes.

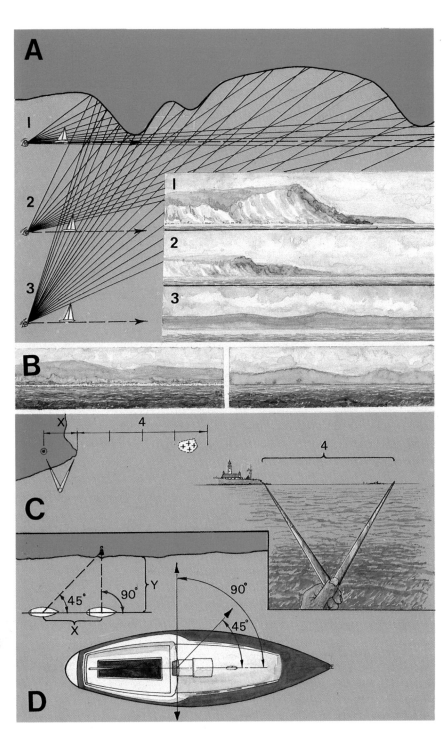

Judging distance off

E. The land from the sea. (1) At 1–2 miles windows have shape, vehicles are seen moving and human figures are dots. (2) At 3 miles windows are seen as dots and human figures are not visible except in clear light. (3) At 5 miles, hedges and individual trees are just distinguishable but houses have no detail. Colours become greyish. (4) At 10 miles houses appear as dots and fields, woods etc are seen in light/dark tones. A wooded skyline has a nibbled appearance. (5) At 20 miles land appears as a dark blue-grey smear, paler at sea level but the tones vary with the angle of sunlight. Inland hills may dominate coastal shape.

The human figure.
100 yards (90 metres) Face a pale oval, dark dash for eyebrows, person recognisable.
200 yards (180 metres) Face a pale blur.
300 yards (270 metres) Face barely discernable.
400 yards (360 metres) Face not visible, walking and leg movement visible.
500 yards (450 metres) Human figure a dark vertical dash.
1 mile Human figure a dot.

F. Rough distance off. The width of an average male fist at arm's length and the distance between eye and fist are on a ratio of 1:7. Identify two landmarks from the chart and as they come abeam measure the distance between them in 'fists'. The example shows them to be $3\frac{1}{2}$ fists apart. The landmarks are $1\frac{1}{2}$ miles apart on the chart therefore: 7 divided by $3\frac{1}{2} = 2$ and $1\frac{1}{2} \times 2 =$ distance off 3 miles.

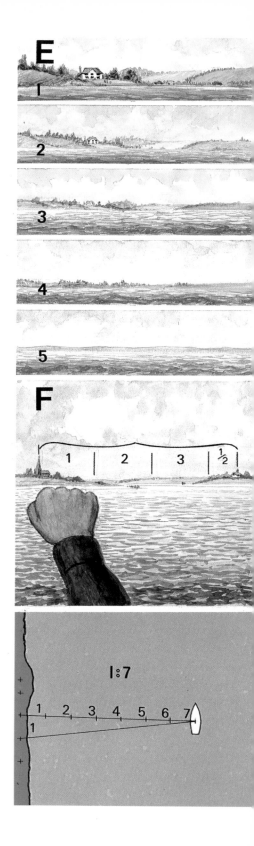

Approaching a landfall in Fijian waters, watching a fringe of palm trees and coral sand rise above the horizon may be a romantic dream, but the art of pilotage by eye is exactly the same when the landfall is one of factory chimneys and breakwaters. Time spent just staring is time well spent.

Coasting complications
– Fishing craft

It is very important for a navigator to know and recognize the lights commonly carried by other vessels. He should also have ready at hand up-to-date information concerning less commonly met lights, such as vessels under tow, unusual vessels and their manoeuvres and in particular the lights used by fishing craft, which when fishing have special rights of way. In different regions there are many types of fishing boat and only some common types are shown here.

The confusion of white and coloured lights which a cruising yacht may meet call for careful action and the fact that fishermen do not always display their lights accurately or clearly must be allowed for. It is not only the vessels which must be avoided however: lines and nets may extend far beyond a vessel and the direction of the gear is (or should be) indicated by the arrangement of her lights.

At (1), a drifter indicates the direction and distance of her nets by a lower white light. (2), pair-trawlers may indicate their gear by means of searchlights. (3), a ground trawler will be moving ahead or she may be stationary hauling her net. The pair trawlers, (2), showing green over white lights, are hauling their gear but the single trawler is under way and showing also her sidelights. Small crabbers, (4), work during daylight, using day signals (day signals apply to all fishing craft and must be learned) and while shooting their long lines of connected pots they must be given absolute right of way.

Coasting complications
– Current inset

In seas where tidal streams prevail, it is often possible to be set close inshore without realising it, especially in hazy weather. This is due to strong local insets of the stream at certain stages of the tide. At **E**, the cruiser is on a safe course to pass outside the buoy some miles away across the bay. At **F** a strong tidal inset is running and although the crew continue to steer their safe course, the cruiser has been set well *inside* it. In clear weather this fact would soon be noticed but haze prevents the use of shore bearings and alternatives such as radio direction finding, cannot always be trusted so close to land, due to the bending of radio waves. Insets vary in strength and cannot easily be predicted.

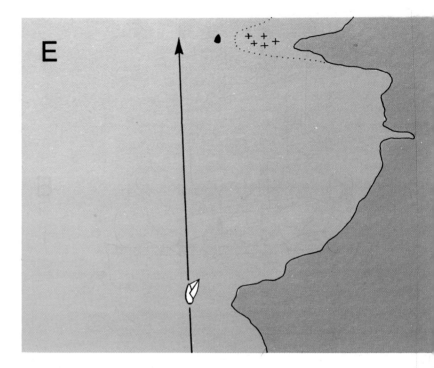

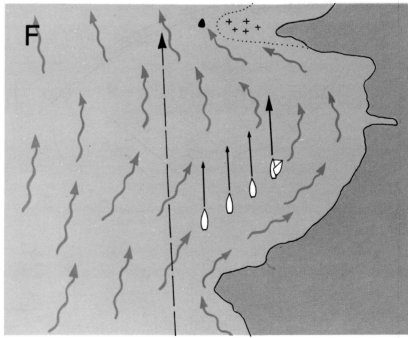

Coasting complications
– Haze

Coastal haze may be due to natural causes or to industrial air pollution and it may be quite local. In clear conditions the port **A** might be entered easily by lining up the church with the harbour beacon but in haze, **B**, the church has been lost to view, but a hilltop building might be mistakenly identified as the church spire.

A navigator's circle of visibility when approaching the coast, **C** is likely to be a narrow one and the view **D** could as easily apply to (1), (2) or (3). Try to estimate just how far you can see by dropping overboard a ball of newspaper and watching it disappear astern, but remember to allow for possible variations in the density of the haze.

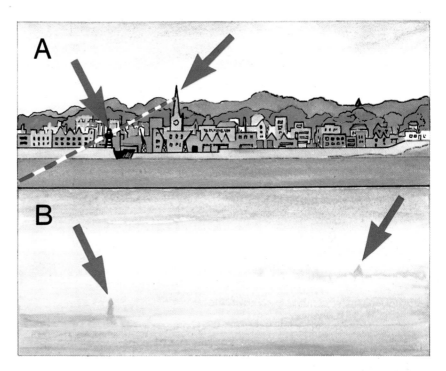

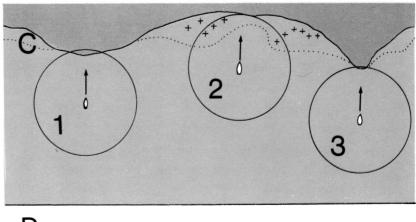

The coastal passage –
Temporary anchorage

After anchoring, select shore marks
which are in line with each other or
take careful compass bearings so that
it can be detected if the anchor is
dragging. With a change of current
or a shift of wind, new marks and
bearings should be found. If the
yacht is swinging around or alternatively moving ahead and astern as
her anchor chain rises and falls, the
marks will tend to alter slightly.

Should she be caught in an open
anchorage by a shift and an increase
of wind, it may prove very difficult to
recover the anchor unless a windlass
is fitted. Usually the engine is used
to motor up to the anchor but should
the engine fail, the anchor will have
to be *sailed* out.

This is done by making sail, suitably reefed, and laying off closehauled. The anchor cable will be dragged across the seabed until its increasing load prevents the yacht from going further. Before this happens she is tacked and her new tack will take her roughly in the direction of her anchor but this time she will be trailing slack cable over the seabed. The most experienced man aboard should be forward to haul in slack as fast as he can while watching the cable. The instant it begins to grow taut, indicating that the anchor is close ahead, he must take a rapid, safe turn around cleat or bitts. The jerk will be dangerously heavy in much wind but it will snatch the anchor out of the seabed. An inexperienced hand must *not* attempt this job unless the weather is moderate.

Exploring tidal rivers

Banks in the delta mouth of river **A** may shift in winter gales and up to date information is important. There will be fast currents in the upper reaches. Bottle neck entrance **B** is dangerous in onshore weather, on the ebb and the range of tide far inland at (**Y**) may be far less than at the mouth (**X**). River **C** has a bar, perhaps navigable for a short while around high tide. Highly dangerous in strong onshore winds.

D. Typical shallow river. Note shallows projecting at river bends (1) marked by withies, (2) an extending bank where the river widens and creates a trap and (3) a creek with a mud spit across the entrance. Mud spit (4) has a withy set well back from the tip; don't round it too closely. At the 'Horse' or mid-channel bank (5), give the withies a wide berth. At (6) the river narrows and deepens; the current is much stronger.

E1 When wind and current are together X-Y. The strongest current follows the deepest water and the channel may be indicated by a smoother slick – faster moving surface makes the apparent wind speed less. **E2**. Wind and current opposing. Choppier wavelets may indicate the deepest water where the apparent wind speed on faster current is greater.

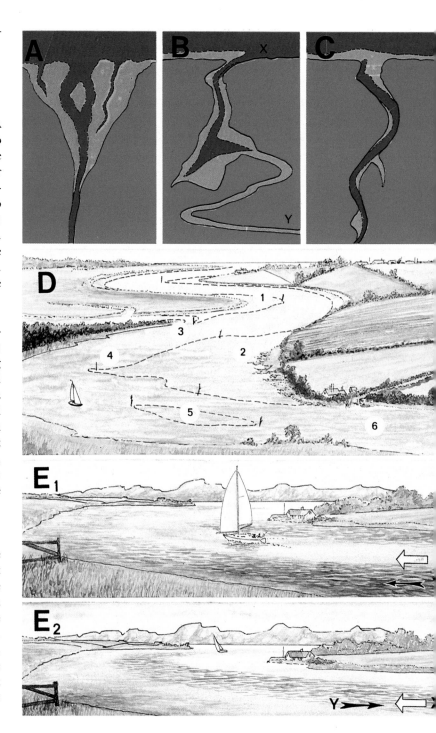

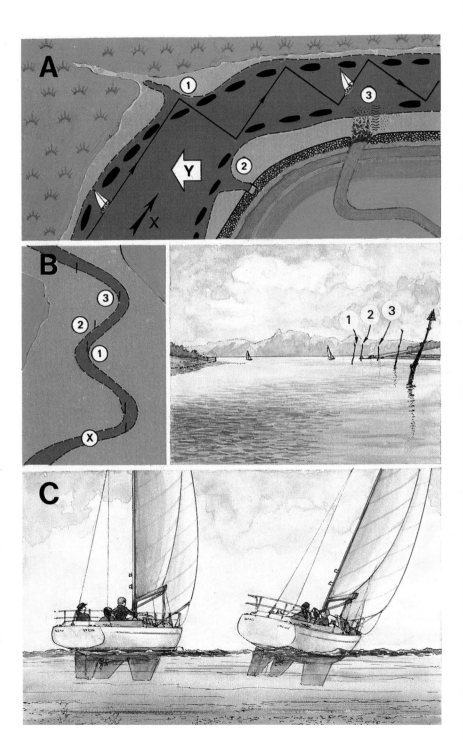

A. Tacking with the current (X) against the wind (Y), the helmsman must beware (1 & 2) where a creek and culvert make deeper inlets. Using the echosounder and dodging moored craft he may sail on too far before tacking and thus run aground. The submerged end of the hard (3) should have a withy on the end but this is missing. A helmsman should notice the ripples but the lane or track is also a clue.

B. In wide, shallow rivers the deep water channel may be very sinuous and withies may be placed on different sides of bends causing confusion. Viewed from X on the chart, withies 1-2-3 appear easy to follow but from sea level the angles are distorted and it would be easy to pass on the wrong side.

C. In shallow water, twin keel yachts when upright are vulnerable to running aground since they cannot then be heeled to reduce draft in the ordinary way. An artificially induced heel of a few degrees to immerse one keel more deeply than the other is an asset if she grounds. Allowing her to come upright then reduces draft marginally.

113

Exploring tidal rivers

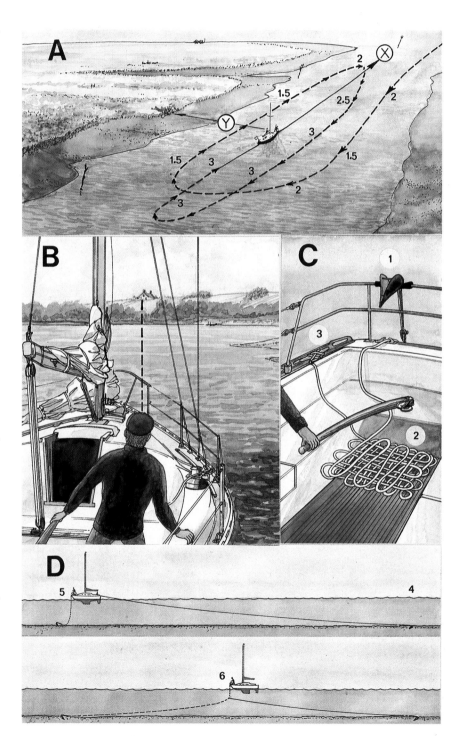

A. Mooring by two anchors in a narrow, shallow creek. The yacht approaches along the arrowed, pecked line, surveying depths by echosounder on both sides of the creek to determine least depths. The deepest water is found in soundings of 3 metres. The crew look for useful shore transits which might give an approach line (**X**) and a rough beam bearing (**Y**, perhaps a prominent tussock of grass) to indicate the spot where the yacht will finally bring up.

B. With the main anchor ready to let go and kedge and warp ready on the stern the yacht is brought on line by means of the bow bearing (a house above a gap in trees). The kedge will be let go astern and half the scope of cable should be out as the beam mark comes to bear.

C. The kedge can be hung over the padded after pulpit rail (1) with its warp leading in to the cockpit sole. It is not coiled but flaked criss-crossed for smooth running (2). The bottom and final end of the warp is made fast securely to a cleat (3). The length of the warp is double the actual length required for the depth of water plus a few extra metres to allow for anchor drag as it bites in.

D. The kedge is let go (at 4) while the yacht motors ahead until she is stop-

ped dead at the end of the (double-length) warp (5); the jerk ensures that the kedge is properly dug in. The main bow anchor must be let go at the precise moment when the yacht ceases to move ahead. By hauling back on the kedge while paying out bow anchor scope, the yacht can be centred between both anchors (6). The kedge warp can then (if desired) be hitched to the main cable. Letting go a couple of metres then takes both cables below the yacht's keel so that she can swing.

On a hazy summer morning the tortuous course of the creek (above) can be studied, but it would take good local knowledge to find it at high tide. This is twin-keeler country, centre-boarder waters where taking the mud is commonplace. Strangers must be sure that they have a level patch of seabed below them though, before taking the ground.

Confined waters
– Handling in wind and current

A. Tacking up a channel with no or only slight current. (1) A cruiser tacks to gain an unobstructed next leg rather than follow dotted line. (2) Luffs a little to avoid stern moorings. Holds on as far as possible thus being able to clear the stern of the anchored vessel on the next tack.

B. Current against wind. (1) Luffs to carry between moored craft, then tacks and bears off to crab across current keeping out of dead-wind area to leeward of vessel. (2) Hangs on current to get clear and tacks to avoid bows of moored craft. (3) Tacks rather than stand on between narrows.

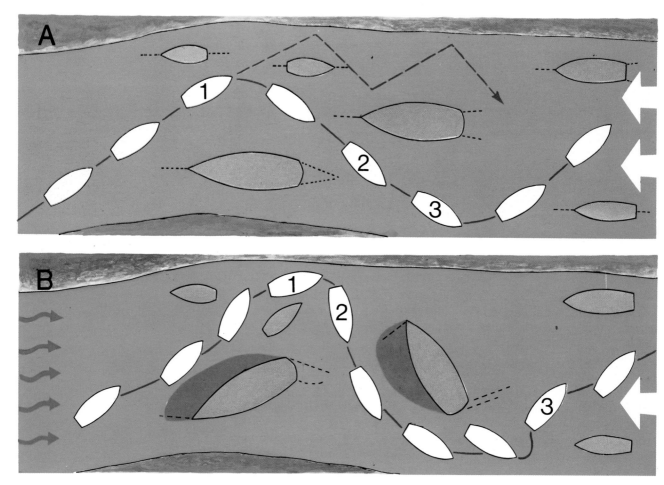

C. (1) Can shave close down current of anchored vessel as she will be heeling away from it and the bow cable will be slack. Tacks short rather than work between anchored craft and (2), luffs well clear of and around the pier end. (3) and (4), short tacks to avoid dead-wind area to leeward of wharfs and vessels.

D. Here the current and wind are together. (1) Tacks in bare time to avoid losing wind under pier. (2) Luffs round pier head and continues as in **C.**

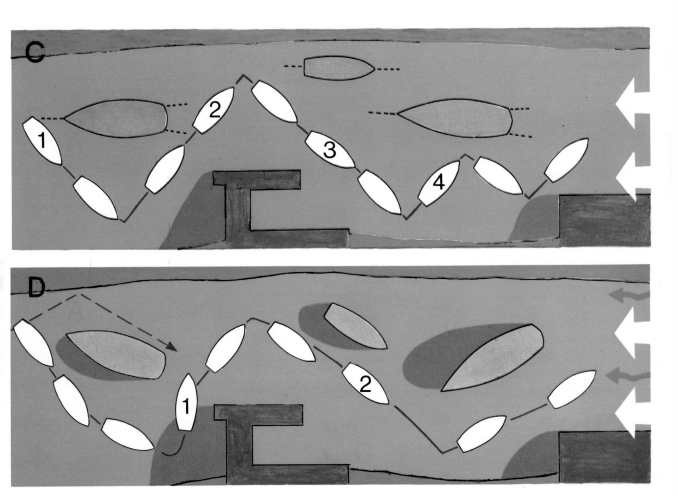

River bars and shallows

1 Viewed from seaward a breaking bar may look harmless but when seen from the land **2**, the true state of the breaking water can be appreciated. Lacking local knowledge or a local pilot, don't attempt to run a bar if it appears to be breaking. The best time to take a bar is usually between half flood and high tide and the worst time is around half-ebb.

An auxiliary sail cruiser is perhaps the worst type of design for shallow water surf, lacking the speed to run in between crests and having a keel which could be vulnerable on the bar, when deep in a water trough. The risk of being rolled or pitchpoled is also greater.

Upon arrival off a bar, note whether there is a swell running in from seaward; a long swell may pass unnoticed at sea but in meeting shoal water it steepens and becomes faster moving. Wind driven onshore waves may not in themselves constitute a bar hazard but combined with a swell they may become so. Bars do not always break continuously. Sometimes, many minutes may go by between heavy breaking seas. For this reason an apparently quiet bar may be a killer in disguise. Stand off in deep water and watch for ten minutes or so. If any doubt, signal for a pilot or make for some safer haven.

Once the run in has been started there is no going back. The sight of a big, breaking sea astern is demoralizing, but to attempt to turn back into it is highly dangerous.

Crossing offlying shallows poses similar problems although there is usually less reason for so doing. If there is a deeper channel over the shallows, remember that it may have shifted and if it is not buoyed proceed slowly on echo-sounder, steering a serpentine course in order to feel out the lie of the shallower water on either side. The aim is to know in which direction you must head should you bump bottom. The presence of current can also show roughly how it lies, the water appearing smoother when wind and current combine, slightly rougher when they oppose.

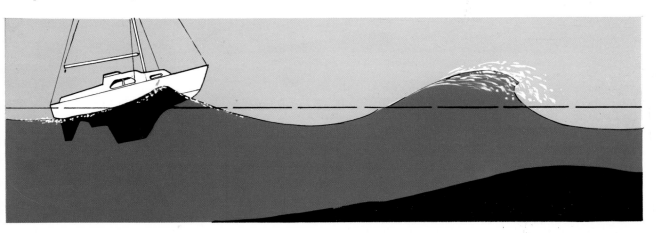

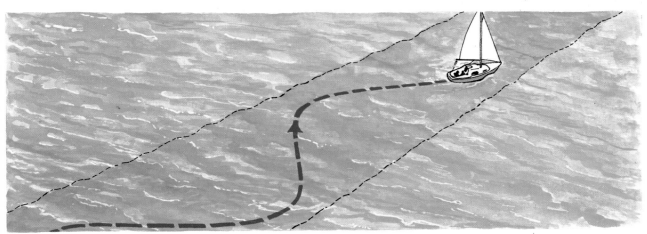

119

Calculating depth

Before approaching a bar or a shoal you must know what depth of water you can expect to find at its shallowest part. Remember though, strong prevailing winds and barometic pressure can alter the height of water in a tidal estuary.

A simple, safe method is to take several position fixes on the approach, noting depth found at each position against depth shown on the chart. In the drawing, a yacht is heading in on leading or range marks. A fix at **A** and a sounding shows 7 metres depth by echo-sounder and 5 metres on the chart. At **B** she finds 5 metres (chart 3 metres). Thus, with a difference to expect of 2 metres, the depth at **C** on the 1 metre shoal should be a total 3 metres.

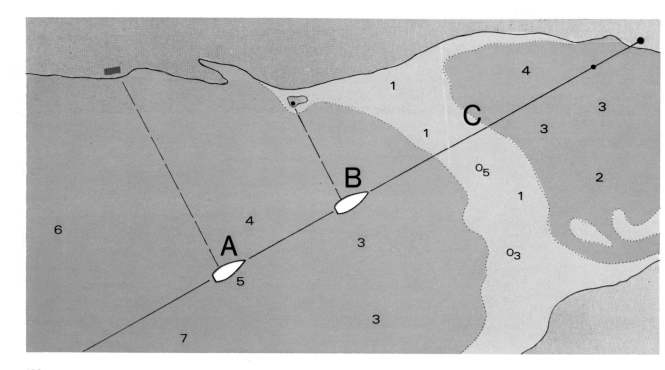

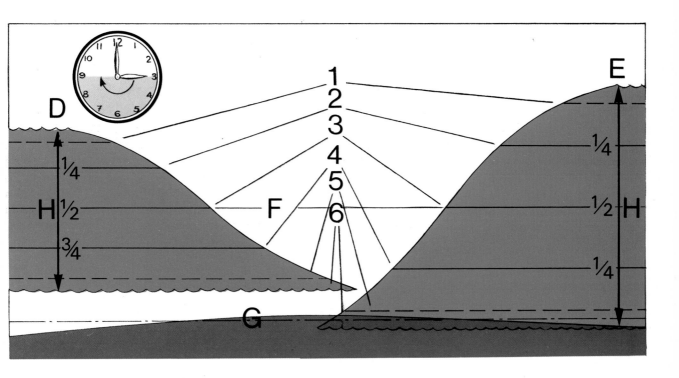

In the diagram:

D = Neap Tide
E = Spring Tide
F = Mean Tide Level
G = Chart Datum

In rough terms, a tide will rise (or fall) its full range in 6 hours (actually a little more). One quarter of this movement in the first two hours and one quarter in the last two hours and the remaining half of the total movement during the middle third and fourth hours. Thus the level changes rapidly during the middle of the tide.

Note that Low Water Springs is considerably lower than Low Water Neaps.

First find the day's RANGE (height of the day's low water from the day's high water equals Range). Another method is to take Mean Level × 2 minus Rise for that day as approximate Range.

The height of low water can be found by subtracting Range from Rise. Depth at any state of tide will now be found approximately as follows:

Example: 2 hours ebb at Neaps will leave three quarters of Range, plus height of low water above Chart Datum, plus chart soundings below Chart Datum.

Remember, at half tide (Mean Tide Level) the depth is the same at Springs as it is at Neaps. At low water Neaps there will be more actual depth than there will be at low water Springs.

121

Fog

Sometimes there is due warning of seafog, but not invariably. The arrival of a warm airstream in the advance of a suddenly deepening depression can bring fog. Usually fog is associated with calm weather and smooth seas – tempting to the passage-maker who gets well out to sea and then encounters dense fog, as he travels in an anti-cyclone, or area of high pressure.

Fog may be dense or patchy, shallow or deep, local or wide-spread, but common to all types is the distortion of sound, thus a ship's siren cannot be relied upon as an indication of distance away or of direction. Collision at sea becomes a great risk and yachts should try to get clear of main shipping routes and, if it is safe to do so, into shallow waters. Big ships will be intent upon avoiding each other and a small yacht can pass unnoticed.

At **A** local radiation fog may fill hollows, river valleys and low ground while remaining clear at sea. It usually disperses with the rising of the sun. The true sea fog, **B**, may be seen as a whitening of the horizon as the banks roll in. It may be extensive or there may be clear lanes between banks. At night, a yacht may be in clear air under a clear sky while all around her ship's sirens are sounding. The warm air stream in advance of a depression can mean both fog and strong winds, **C**, a very dangerous combination and one in which the radar signal returned by a small yacht labouring among big seas is likely to be small and uncertain.

Fog tactics

Avoid shipping lanes. If caught in one when fog descends, cross at right angles, show a radar reflector, sound your fog horn and maintain keen listening watch forward. Keep good steerage way on and all crew to wear lifejackets but not harnesses. If possible tow the dinghy. Don't suppose any ship's siren to be on your safe side because fog bends sound waves, muffles or amplifies them. *Any* other vessel is dangerous to you. Two big ships may be passing safely but then one, making an emergency evasive turn, may endanger you. If under engine you may have to throttle back at intervals in order to listen.

In very thick fog the reed of an aerosol type fog horn has a tendency to 'freeze' and lose power. Carry a mouth horn as well. Sound it evenly in all directions but not towards your crew or they will be temporarily deafened.

The aim should be to make for shallow water. Study the chart carefully in case your navigation is amiss and deep water extends close inshore to a rocky coast.

In fog, the first glimpse of a ship bearing down may be her white bow wave, or if the fog is thicker at sea level, her white bridge, although sometimes dark shapes show up first. You will have seconds in which to estimate her course angle relative to your own. Turning by bearing away may give you extra seconds.

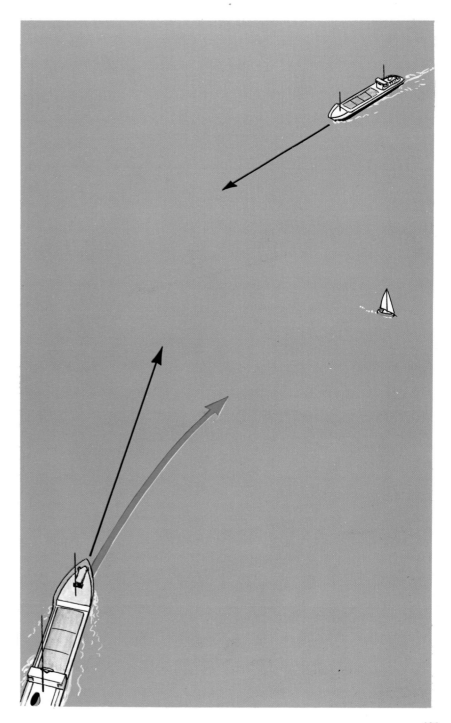

Fog
– the radar reflector

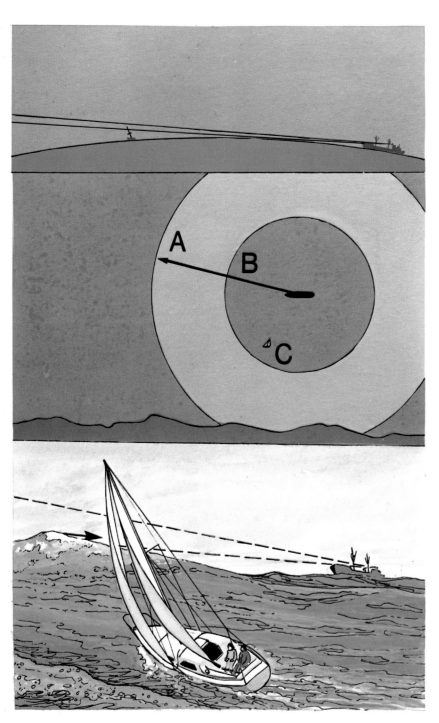

This is why a metal mast will only return a good signal during the brief moments when it is at 90 degrees to the radar beam and a patchy 'blip' on the radar screen is the result. Don't rely upon your boat giving a steady echo in a seaway. Her gyrations plus the clutter of reflected wave crests may pass unnoticed. Moreover, the radar operator may not be paying full attention, or he may be using it at maximum range and miss an object close to. Sophisticated equipment expertly used may not miss you, but this cannot be taken for granted.

Horizon dip may hide the hull of a yacht. The ship using full range **A** may miss the yacht **C** which is inside the short range **B** and a deep wave trough may blanket a small vessel so frequently that any return signal she gives might be dismissed as floating debris.

A radar signal is similar to a beam of light. It cannot bend around corners and a radar reflector with a surface placed at 90 degrees to the signal, like a mirror, will return the signal (1), (2) and (3) show how a beam of light from a torch is either deflected (1), or returned (2). If a group of mirrors (3), all at 90 degrees to each other, is used the beam 'bounces' from one to another and then is returned. The familiar octahedral radar reflector is designed on this principle. No matter what angle it is to the radar signal, the signal will be reflected back.

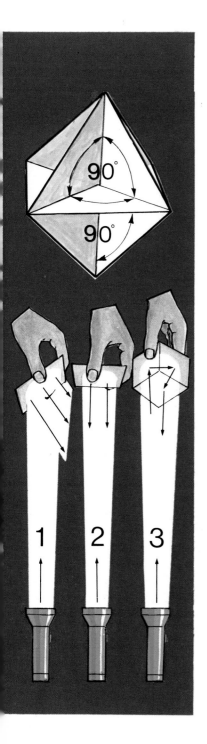

125

Fog
– the radar reflector

Every cruiser using waters frequented by big ships should have a permanently fitted radar reflector.

(1). The best position is at the masthead where it is at maximum height and not hidden by sails. (2). A minimum height above sea level of 10 feet must be sought or it will be below the horizon at long ranges. (3). A bow staff is a useful compromise, permitting an extra large reflector to be displayed in really dangerous situations. (4). Hoisted to the spreader a reflector bangs around unless it is also clipped to a stay.

The correct angle may be found by standing the reflector flat on deck. This is the 'catch-water' position.

The larger the reflector the better, the signal increasing by the square of the area. The argument that a small reflector of 1 ft corner to corner measurement is acceptable as half the value of a 2 ft one, and therefore suitable for a very small boat, is quite wrong – it would be many, many times less efficient. An 18 inch reflector is the minimum size for a permanent fitting. The angles of the plates must be exactly 90 degrees. Even errors of 3 degrees can cause a 50 per cent loss of efficiency.

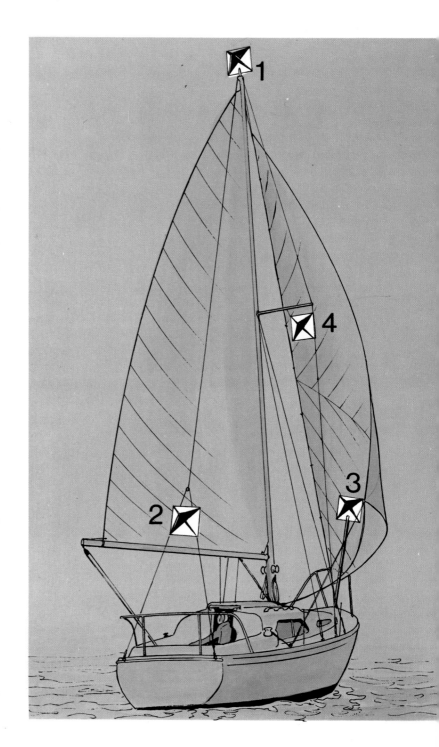

Sea state

Remember, that ability to cope with rough weather is not just a question of the sort of boat you own but also having the crew stamina to keep going for as long as may be necessary.

The following is based upon the Beaufort Scale.

Force 2 4–6 knots, wave height 0.4 metre. Light breeze, wavelets and gentle sailing.

Force 3 7–10 knots, wave height 0.4 metre. Gentle breeze, large wavelets with occasional small crests. Cruisers heel.

Force 4 11–16 knots, wave height 1 metre. Moderate breeze, waves lengthening, excellent sailing but may need one reef.

Force 5 17–21 knots, wave height 2 metres. Fresh breeze, moderate and more pronounced waves with many white crests, maybe spray. Small jib, double reef, heavy going to windward.

Force 7 28–33 knots, wave height up to 4 metres. Heaping waves with foam streaks beginning. Small cruisers make for shelter. Deeply reefed mainsail, storm jib or main and engine.

Force 8 34–40 knots, wave height 5.5 metres. Gale. Waves longer, crests blowing in spindrift, long foam streaks. Small cruisers may abandon passage in favour of survival tactics.

Force 10 48–55 knots, wave height 9 metres. Storm. High overhanging crests, sea white with dense foam and spindrift affecting visibility. Survival tactics.

Sea state

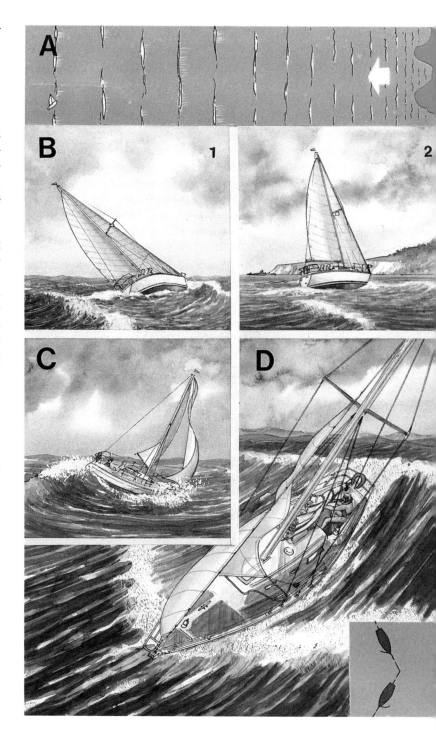

A. Waves increase in size for a given wind strength in accordance with distance from sheltering land. The distance is known as 'the fetch'. Currents, depths and seabed contours further alter the wave patterns.

B. For a given wind speed a yacht at sea in rough water may be heavily overpressed (1), yet in the same wind strength and under the same sail area but under the shelter of land she may be sailing easily (2). This is one of the easiest ways to be caught out at the start of a passage when leaving shelter. Running before a rising wind constitutes a worse problem.

C. A classic emergency can arise in a lightly crewed boat on a dead run in strengthening wind. The skipper may be the only person capable of steering – the skipper may also be the only navigator aboard. He or she may also be the only person who knows how to reef.

D. Running under jib only. At intervals the sail flogs with great violence and may damage either itself or something else. It is better to run in a series of shallow down-wind tacks of equal length. In rough (but not survival) conditions use of engine at low revs may give better control.

Broad reaching under spinnaker in sheltered water is a delight but those clouds could deliver a squall or two and smart sail handling may be called for. The helmsman would have to bear away so that the spinnaker was blanketed by the mainsail in order to lower it safely and he will keep an eye to windward for squalls and to leeward for sea room to bear off should this be needed.

Seeking shelter

Emergency shelter in bad weather and temporary shelter while waiting out a foul tide may need to be sought while cruising. Shelter from the wind, however, is not necessarily comfortable shelter or even safe. Waves bend as they pass along the land's edge, curving round and affecting open bays.

At (1), the island offers tenuous shelter for a short stay provided the yacht can lie close in shore and the bay, (2), may also remain quiet and clear of the wave pattern provided the wind does not shift and blow into it. The island, (3), however offers no shelter, neither does the shallow bay (5). The small enclosed bay, (4), is

dangerous because a shift of wind could well trap the yacht sheltering there.

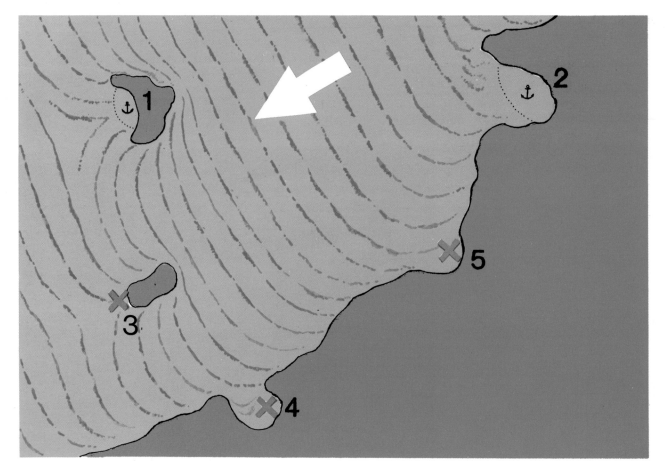

At **A** and **B** the two anchorages would offer shelter from the prevailing wind but should the wind change suddenly and blow onshore, **B** would prove to be a trap. Bay **A** on the other hand, would allow the yacht an easy escape on either port or starboard tack. Escape under sail should always be the objective for any vessel with sail as her main propulsion; the use of engine power is a bonus.

In seeking temporary anchorages note the weather trend existing and the local area forecast and barometer (if applicable to conditions in the area). Always keep the crew and vessel in a state of readiness for instant departure, plot a safe compass course for escape and maintain a running watch.

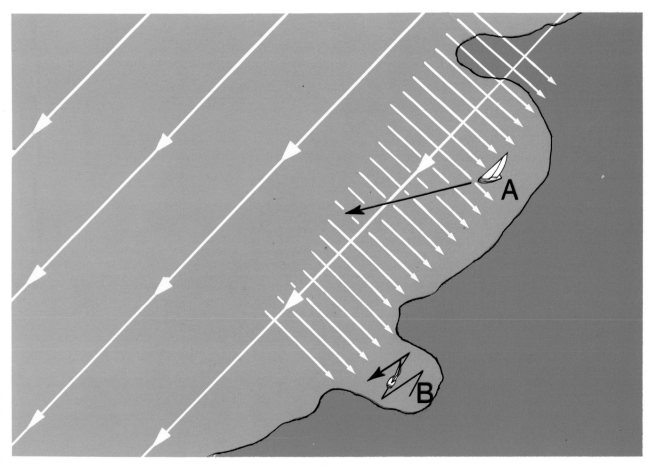

Making for shelter

A low pressure system can travel forward at 20–25 knots, which means that if it is 200 miles away (for example) only about 8 hours remain in which to make shelter. During this time winds may rise rapidly to gale force and visibility may decrease. A small cruiser at sea may be run for shelter or she may be taken further seaward to gain a safer offing. This is the choice.

If we assumed that the boats at **E**, **F**, **G**, **H**, **J**, and **L** can all make 5 knots, boats **E**, **F** and **G** might make for the sheltering land to windward. **E** and **F** might manage it. Boat **H** is trying to get a safer offing to seaward but boat **J** is undecided. She is 40 miles from shelter but like **K** and **L** (20 and 30 miles from it), she might not get there before visibility closes down. The wise decision might be for **J** to make to seaward.

Winds can and do shift direction during a gale. This must be considered and contingency plans made.

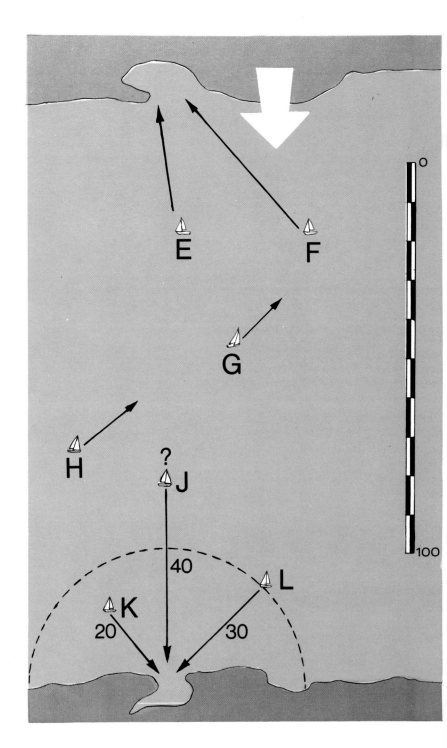

Bad weather and the crew

The new-comer to sailboat cruising should try to avoid bad weather until such time as he is competent to handle and navigate his boat in those conditions. He would be wise to gain his bad weather experience, if he can, by sailing as crew in a well handled boat, under an experienced skipper. It isn't always possible to avoid bad weather but you can read and think about it and you can make sure that your boat is equipped for it.

A calm sea poses few problems. The wind is the culprit and the sea is obedient to it. Study the wind and you have the secrets of the waves.

Strong winds and rough water are the ultimate test of man and boat. Any weakness in either promotes further strain and searches out new weaknesses. Violent motion, noise and fatigue make even simple jobs complicated and simple navigation difficult. Seasickness may impose even more strain. Learn your job so thoroughly in fine weather that the habit and instinct for doing things right will become second nature to you.

A boat with reliable engine, gear and sails needs a minimum of attention in bad weather. Proper stowage below prevents chaos and a good chart table with a safe stowage for books and instruments makes navigation far easier for a tired man. Ship-to-shore radio and an awareness that advice and help if needed are readily available, eases mental strain and reduces worry.

A Force 5–6 wind (17–27 knots) can produce a sea which can reduce crew strength seriously and it doesn't take a gale to cause trouble. The 34–40 knots of gale force is nearly double the force of a fresh to strong breeze but many beginners *think* that they have been out in gale force winds simply because a gale was forecast for their area at that time.

A Force 8 gale is a solid blast of wind and water and it can quickly develop into Storm Force 9–10 which is almost half as strong again. Small yachts can and regularly do survive, provided their crews keep their heads. A good boat and gear, open water and searoom to leeward are the essentials. Read all accounts of how other people fared, what they did and the mistakes they made. Don't make a panic dash for unsuitable shelter. Usually it is the crew that wrecks the boat – not the boat that fails her crew. Accept the fact that in a small sailing cruiser, crew strength will be reduced to one or two people by bad weather and plan accordingly. Be optimistic, keep up morale and don't give up.

Bad weather dangers

The waves and the land are the threats. Big ocean waves are not usually dangerous to small craft unless the cross sea of a wind change or some other phenomenon causes a big wave to rear and to break heavily aboard. Closer to land however a shallowing of the seabed **A** or strong currents off headlands **B** cause big seas to become shorter and steeper, liable to break.

Shallow water and/or an ebb current at a river mouth can render it dangerous to enter in bad weather **C** and a lee shore haven **D** which is difficult to find can be suicidal when visibility has closed down to a few hundred yards – the slightest navigational error can then be fatal.

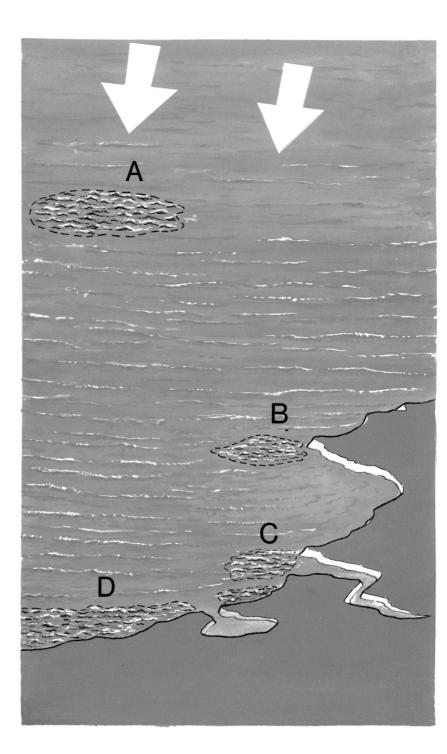

Land and sea

The duration of a gale greatly depends upon local weather patterns. It may be a few hours brought about by the excessive sea breeze in a hot climate, or even several days when consequent upon other factors. A chain of depressions may cause a succession of gales interspersed by wind shifts and lulls.

A. Drifting at 3 knots, boat (x) has about 24 hours and boat (y) has 48 hours before the lee shore threatens them. When the duration of a gale is unknown, every mile of searoom is vital.

Waves can overwhelm a boat. The rogue wave **B** is a possible open sea danger, but a lesser one than the tide rip with its dangerous confusion of pyramidal waves. Poor visibility **C** poses great risk to a boat close in-shore and making for shelter.

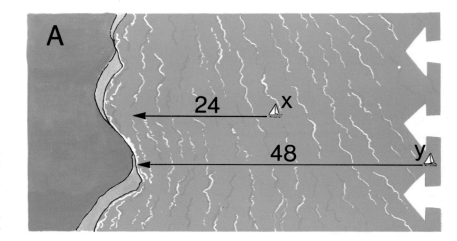

Land and sea

Big waves can become a danger if a boat is run before them too long or too fast. In **D1** and **2** the yacht's wake causes waves to break. She may slew across them beam-on and be rolled over or she may bury her bow deeply and turn stern-over-bow. Damage is certain and very possibly crew may be lost overboard.

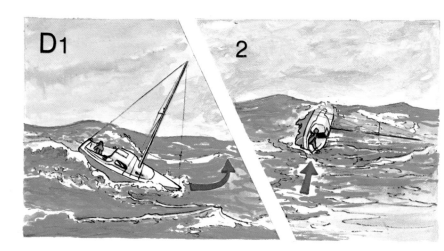

Strength and good design are essential in the following:
(1) Reefing gear.
(2) Cockpit and rate of drainage.
(3) Companionway door or closure.
(4) Mast and rigging.
(5) Size and strength of windows.
(6) Efficiency of ventilators.
(7) Strength and security of fore-hatch.
(8) Height and strength of life-lines and pulpits.

With a quartering breeze and under easy canvas *Sea Wraith* (facing page) is making a fast passage. With a good crew and a well found ship, strong wind sailing should hold no fears. It is better to learn the power of the wind under controlled conditions than to be taught the hard way.

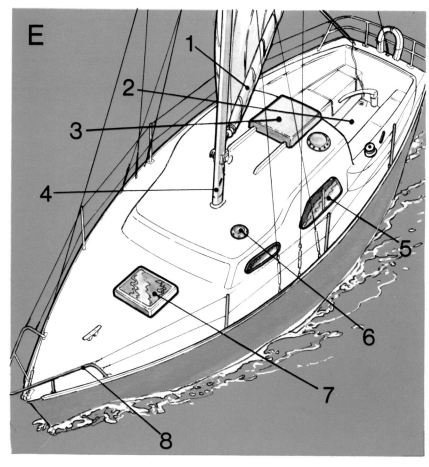

Flooding

Hull openings, hatches and so on can let in great volumes of solid water unless strongly protected. Hatch boards should not be able to slide away or knock down and **A** shows a typically weak arrangement which could push inwards. **B**, with a full moulded recess, is better.

Plastic windows **C** can bulge under pressure and if set in a rubber strip they can flip out altogether. An emergency plywood shutter is a standby in case of trouble.

Many forehatches are secured only by a small bolt and violent pounding can loosen them, allowing them to blow open. A bad weather 'strongback' with a screwed hook engaging in an eye beneath the hatch is a wise precaution, **D**.

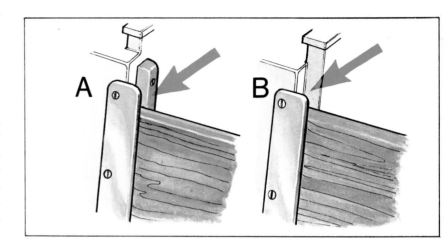

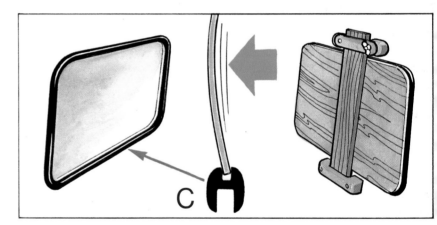

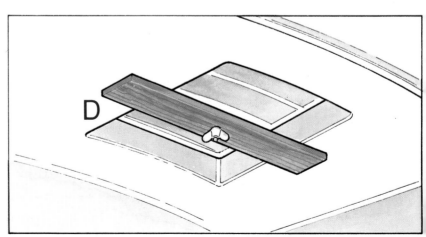

Cockpit

Very few cockpits drain fast enough to rid them of water if swamped, before successive waves arrive. **E**, if the companionway is open, water will pour below and although much of it will be rolled out by the boat's motion, **F** she may remain sluggish and slow to lift her stern to other oncoming waves.

Keep the companionway boards shipped, have a properly fitted bilge pump and have a bucket stowed handy to the cockpit – it is probably the quickest means of emptying a cockpit.

G. If much water has gone below it will be difficult to pump out if the boat is pitching and rolling. It may be safer to turn head to sea and lie hove-to while it is done.

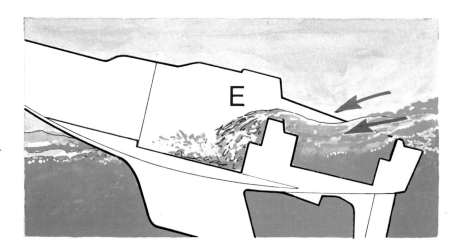

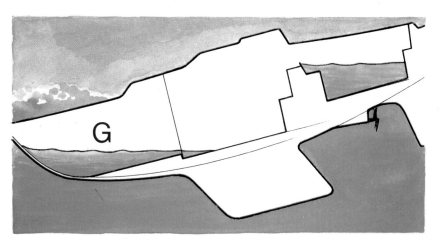

Action

Boats, seas and conditions vary so much that one can only generalize about action to take. Getting an offing is a prime requirement if shelter is not possible.

A. Early, efficient reefing and use of engine to get well clear of lee shores in *good time* may be vital.

B. In a moderate gale situation, heaving-to may suffice, using a properly cut trisail and storm jib for preference. Hove-to, a yacht may ride with some comfort until weather moderates. If it worsens and heavy seas begin breaking aboard other action is needed.

C. Running under bare poles is safe until boat speed reaches near-wave speed, when risk of broaching beam on or being filled from astern exists. The boat must be slowed down before this happens.

D. The accepted action in these conditions is to stream a warp in a large loop or bight. It must be of at least 300 feet length – longer if possible. The drag both causes crests to break well astern and slows forward speed to a safe limit.

In very extreme conditions running with a warp may become dangerous due to risk of a boat being pitchpoled forward or overwhelmed by a crest. A sea anchor (**E**) may offer safety although most modern hulls lying to one from the bow tend to lie beam on.

F. Drifting a'hull, helm lashed amidships and all openings battened down is an extreme measure dependent for safety upon the strength of decks and coachroof etc. Searoom is needed as a boat may drift at a rate of 2–4 knots.

What must be appreciated, is that whatever course of action is adopted, the combined effects of wild motion, noise and fatigue render even the simplest of tasks extremely difficult. It is all too easy to slip into a lethargic state of mind and to do nothing, or delay until it is too late.

Emergency equipment

Certain emergency equipment for seagoing yachts is recommended in some countries and required by law in others. The list varies a little but common to all are the essential basics:

(1) Two 3-lb fire extinguishers, regularly tested by the manufacturers.
(2) At least two lifebuoys (see section on man overboard for other essentials).
(3) A powerful torch.
(4) First aid kit.
(5) At least 12 assorted distress signals.
(6) Daylight smoke signals.
(7) Lifejackets for all crew to national or official specifications (e.g. British Standard 3595 or US Coastguard PFD – Personal Flotation Device).
(8) Safety harnesses for all crew.
(9) Engine spanners and other tools.
(10) Navigational lights to official requirements.
(11) Spare fuel in reserve.
(12) Radio Receiver, and VHF radio telephone.

(13) Automatic liferaft.
(14) Powerful wire cutters.
(15) Adequate charts corrected up to date.

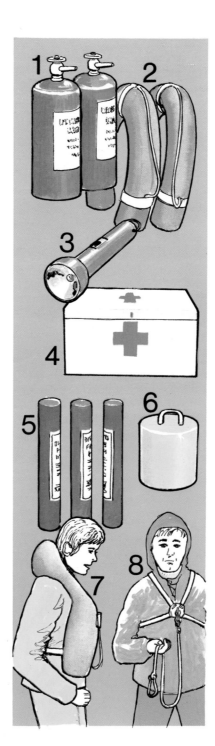

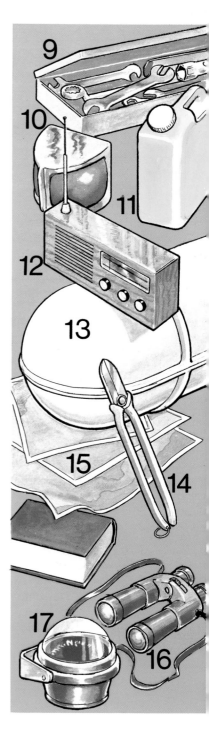

16) Good binoculars suitable for night use.

17) Reliable compass corrected for deviation

The crew must know where all equipment is stowed and how to use it. Extinguishers, torch, safety harnesses, lifejackets, flares and first aid kit must be in plain view.

Fire extinguishers and distress signals cannot be tested and if allowed to become out of date, damp or damaged they will almost certainly fail. Extinguishers are very vulnerable, especially dry powder types. Neither will help if careless use of bottled gas or petrol creates danger of an explosion. Leakage of these is one of the main hazards of life afloat.

Sailing is fun. Proper safety aids and sensible precautions make it more so because the knowledge that a boat is safely sailed is reassuring to the family and friends who are the crew.

When all else fails, a self-inflating liferaft may provide the ultimate escape from tragedy. It is an expensive item of equipment, but can be hired. On an offshore passage it is a sound assurance. The liferaft should be stowed within easy reach of the cockpit to allow almost instant launching.

Rescue

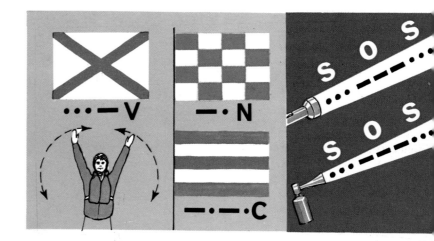

Code flag V (I require assistance) is not a distress signal and it is used when a tow is needed, to borrow fuel etc. Arm waving, as shown, means help needed, maybe an emergency. Code flags NC (or flashed or sounded on a fog horn) are used in distress, also SOS. Code word MAY-DAY is the radio telephone distress signal.

Use distress pyrotechnics wisely. Altitude rockets are wasted if there is low cloud. Hand flares used in inflatable craft can drop burning cinder which could damage the fabric. Use flares in twos. Hold to leeward and don't look at them. A watcher may half-see the first but he will be ready for the second and might otherwise have thought he'd imagined it. You may have to wait for hours – have you enough signals? A yellow day smoke signal is a valuable aid to a searching helicopter.

Helicopter rescue

The mast of a rolling, pitching yacht makes it dangerous to lower a man on board. If the wire becomes entangled or if it is made fast, it can crash the aircraft. If possible clear away the backstay and with all sails down, motor slowly head to wind. If none of this is possible, yacht crew in lifejackets must be prepared to jump overboard one at a time to be picked up.

Better still, stream the dinghy downwind on a long line. If an injured crew member is to be flown off, send someone with him. If he has been given drugs or a tourniquet applied, send a message with him giving details and time at which the tourniquet was applied. Do as instructed: the helicopter crew are specialists.

Towing at Sea

A. Prepare by hauling in any trailing ropes or wires that might foul a rescuer's propeller, then lash any loose gear on deck and clear it as much as possible in readiness for towing. See that everybody is wearing a lifejacket. Fairleads and cleats are sometimes too small and sharp-edged to bear heavy loads, if so, pad the bow fairlead and make provision for lashing the towrope into it so that it cannot jump out.

B. If the foredeck cleat looks inadequate, the mast step on deck (1), can sometimes be used, provided the pull is kept low by lashings. Don't tow from the mast unless it is keel-stepped. Alternatively a warp can be taken back round the quarter cleats (2). This can be dangerous if they are inadequate since the warp could sweep forward across the cockpit if they failed. A warp round the hull (3) can also be used provided the stern doesn't rake forward (inset). It must be supported at intervals outside the deck edge.

C. The middle of the tow should not lift from the water; sufficient length or weight ensures this. Sometimes the tow can be attached to the anchor chain.

D. The yacht may be lying beam-on to the sea. If the tow will be to windward the towing vessel must start with

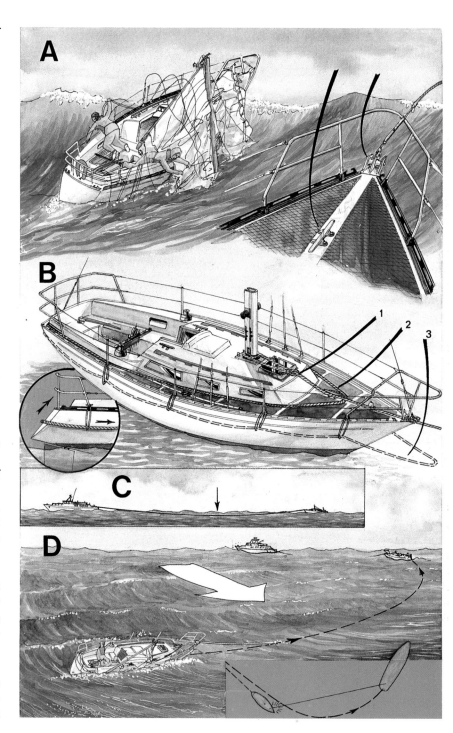

a wide turn, otherwise (inset) the warp may jump the fairlead and part the forestay, if the mast is still standing.

E. In a following sea, the towed yacht may over-run the towrope and the heavy snatch which follows (1), could part the tow. The disabled yacht should stream astern a drag (2), such as a big coil of warps (inset), weighted bunk mattress etc. A drag or drogue is essential if the rudder is damaged.

F. Towing too fast can also lead to sheering out of control and parting of the tow. A lifeboat coxswain will know the correct speed but fishing boat, coaster or other skippers may not.

A lifeboat coxswain will probably put one of his crew aboard the towed yacht who will be effectively in charge. Where other types of vessel provide the tow the yacht skipper should endeavour to take charge and to agree a price for the tow, using his own warp, provided it is adequate. Beware towing by large vessels as their lowest speed may still be dangerously fast.

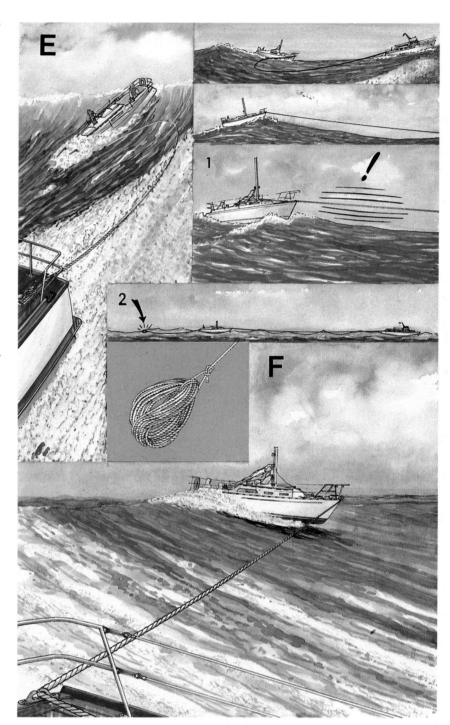

Yachts and shipping

The International Rules for the Prevention of Collision at Sea must be obeyed, but the increasing size of ships makes their ability to take quick avoiding action very difficult. In trying to avoid each other, the yachtsman may be caught in the middle. He must do more than obey the Rules, he must think far ahead because, despite his quick manoeuvrability, his is the slowest vessel at sea.

The illustration shows a dredged deep water channel in the approaches to a busy port, where big ships have an indisputable Right of Way over yachts and small craft. Crossing such a channel calls for judgement of the speed and manoeuvrability of the big ships.

Yacht **A**, planning to cross between ships (w) and (x) will be too close to the bows of (w) and in danger from the approaching (y).

Yacht **B** is crossing obliquely and she will be longer at risk than yacht **C** which is crossing more at right angles and using her engine to get across quickly ahead of ship (z) and well ahead of ship (x).

Yacht **D** bears away under the stern of ship (z) but by mid channel ship (x) will be bearing down on her fast. She must then either gamble on getting across, turn back, or head down the centre of the channel, which may worry the pilot of the ship (x).

The angles of the masts of approaching ships is the yachtsman's guide to their heading but a bend in the channel can be confusing. The yacht **D** has the masts of ship (x) in line and seems to be crossing her safely but by the time she has crossed astern of ship (z), the ship (x) will have altered her course on the bend and she will be on a collision course with the yacht.

Situation **E** shows a yacht in the proximity of two small coasters. The coaster at (1) will have to give way to the coaster at (2). She blows one blast signifying a turn to starboard. The yacht is now at risk unless she too turns to starboard.

Small commercial craft don't always give way to sail. At sea they may be on autopilot with nobody on the lookout for quite long periods. They may also be on radar watch only (big ships also). Make allowances for human error on the bridge and stay clear.

The skipper of this yacht may have judged things to a nicety but he has left no room for error. Those on the bridge of the container ship may not even be aware that the yacht is there and their view ahead may be a quarter mile or more. Never impose a strain on a vessel which is restricted in her manoeuvrability.

The open sea

Big ships cannot stop or alter course quickly. At **A** the ship may take 2–3 miles to stop, even with engines full astern. At **B** the ship is turning hard a'port with her stern swinging far out of line so that while her bows might miss a small vessel, her stern could hit it.

The ship at **C** is making a wide turn on to a new course. The yacht at **D** sees her come bows-on and motors fast to get clear but the ship has not yet settled on her new heading and she is yawing. By the time she is steady **C**2, a collision situation is building up.

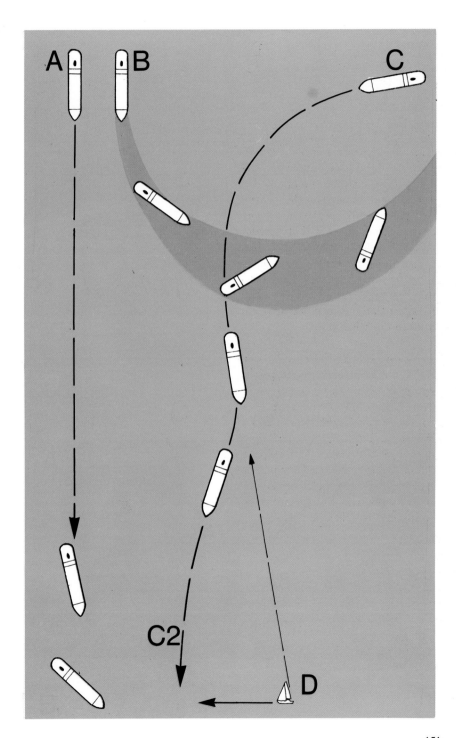

The open sea

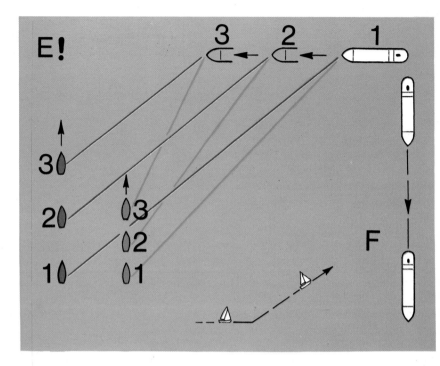

In sketch **E** the red yacht has the ship on a bearing which doesn't alter as the vessels converge – evidence of a collision situation. The green yacht finds that the bearing changes steadily as the two vessels draw nearer, showing that no collision risk exists provided both hold course and speed. At **F** a yacht makes a bold course alteration to avoid a ship, making her intentions plain. Small, erratic course changes can confuse the other vessel.

At **G** ship (y) is in clear view from the yacht and seems to be passing safely but the ship's radar shows ship (x) to be on a converging course with Right of Way. From the deck of the yacht, ship (x) may be hull-down over the horizon. When ship (y) alters course the yachtsman, not knowing why she has done so, may react wrongly. Be prepared for seemingly inexplicable behaviour.

At night

A. Never get close under the bows of big ships, day or night unless quite sure that they are moored or at anchor, there is a blind arc forward of the bows when viewed from the bridge. Remember also, that while a ship's lights are plainly seen by the yachtsman, his own lights, when viewed from high on the bridge, may be lost against and among the waves.

B. If your bows are toward an approaching ship, steer a steady course, even when passing safely. From the bridge your navigation lights may otherwise show red and green alternately as you weave around. This could confuse a simple situation and lead to a dangerous course alteration by the big ship. (1), (2), and (3) show what the big ship sees.

C. Are your lights correctly aligned? Check them before making a night passage. This can be done in a marina by walking around and taking careful bearings of the light sectors.

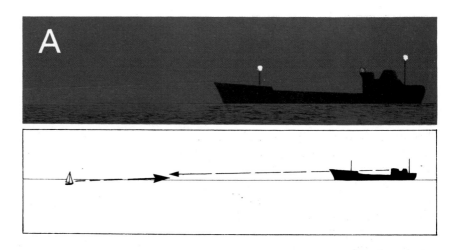

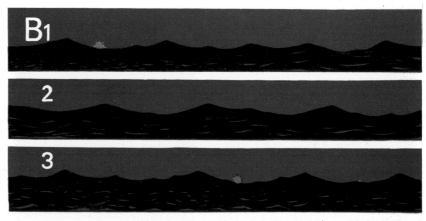

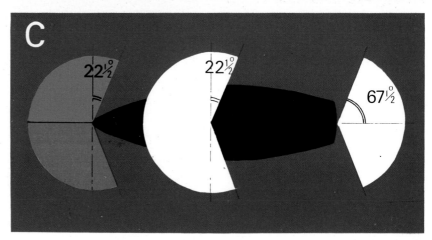

At night

The big ship look-out may not see your lights. If in doubt it is better to switch on *all* lights, including spreader or crosstree lights, even though this may not comply with the requirements for a vessel under sail. BE SEEN.

There should be a powerful flash-light at hand, shine it towards the ship. Watchers will then see a sharp pinpoint of light whereas they might fail to see the diffused glow of a torchbeam shone upon your sail. Hold it steady. If you flash it on and off, watchers may assume that you are trying to send a Morse message. Remain alert until the ship is completely past – she could always make a last minute alteration of course.

The tender

Most cruising yacht tenders today are of an inflatable type, although our sketch on the next page also shows two rigid tenders of plywood or glassfibre construction.

The essentials are that a tender should be light, self-buoyant and of sufficient capacity to carry at least three adults safely in rough water. It should be robust enough to stand up to constant use and easy to row.

Although many owners prefer to use a light outboard motor instead of a pair of oars, these should be carried for emergency use; or at least there should be a paddle. Few inflatables row easily and in a fresh breeze with a full load aboard, it is all too easy to be carried helplessly downwind. When used at night the tender should have a torch aboard for use in case of pending collision or for signalling. Lifejackets should be worn and, ideally there should be a light anchor and line attached to the tender; a bailer of some kind is essential.

Records show an alarmingly high number of fatal accidents involving tenders, especially used at night. Overloading is a prime cause. There is a great temptation to embark from the shore, having managed to pack the whole crew aboard, leaving very little freeboard. Often that which is smooth close to shore, becomes choppy out in the tideway and it is then highly dangerous to either go on or to go back. Better not to start out overloaded.

The tender

At **A** an overloaded tender is being rowed with some difficulty by a man in the bows – the narrower hull at that point reducing his leverage on the oars. The stern is so low in the water that even a small wave can slop aboard. The trim of the boat is also wrong and this will make rowing even harder since the stern will drag and the rower will be pitched up and down, causing him to miss strokes. At **B** the tender is correctly loaded for her size, she is also properly trimmed fore-and-aft, with the rower seated at the most advantageous position.

A good (hard) tender may look like this (lower picture). Notice the buoyancy tanks permanently fixed below the thwarts or seats, the sensible fender around the gunwale and the provision for two rowing positions. With only two people aboard, the rower will need to sit at the forward position in order to trim the tender correctly.

Tender handling

If the cruiser is moored in a strong current, plan to arrive well forward to allow for seconds spent shipping oars before grabbing for the yacht's rail. Secure the tender's painter right away.

Other approaches may be by rowing crab-wise across the current or by dropping down-current towards the moored yacht, allowing the tender to pivot bows to the current while still above the yacht. By rowing to stem the current, the tender can be allowed to sidle in towards the bows of the yacht.

There are fewer problems to using an outboard motor, but an approach while stemming the current is always important. Steer straight alongside at a slight angle, cutting the motor when it is apparent that you are going to carry enough way to get there. Remember a stopped propeller has a dragging effect.

Tender handling

Be strict about the way in which passengers leave the tender. Keep her trimmed and ensure that the first man out takes the painter and holds the bows in while others disembark.

It is unwise to tow any dinghy in a rough sea, especially a following sea, when a hard tender will run up on a wave surge and crash into the parent boat's stern. In more than a moderate breeze an inflatable is liable to flip over. Tow it on a very short scope and first remove all loose gear. It is better to stow it on deck, half deflated and well lashed down.

Transferring crew from a dinghy being towed alongside is risky. Weight in the bows will cause the tender to bury her bows and fill. Keep weight slightly aft of amidships and if transferring from cruiser to dinghy, sit down at once.

Eating and sleeping

Choose mealtimes, not by the clock but when the crew is free to relax and when it will not interrupt the sleep of the watch off duty. Don't serve up just when the ship is about to be worked through a difficult channel – ask the navigator whether any manoeuvres are imminent. To be of value, there must be time to digest a meal properly and calmly.

In weather that is too rough for cooking in safety, boiled eggs, chocolate, cheese, nuts, raisins, fruit and fruit juice offer all the nourishment needed. Drink plenty of liquid because dehydration, especially after seasickness, is a pitfall at sea.

Never hand over the night watch to a newly awakened man. Give him time to become fully alert. During the early stages of a sea passage nobody feels that he has had all the sleep he needs and it may take a full ten minutes before a sleepy man is fully alert.

At the start of a passage don't worry if you cannot sleep, by your next watch below you will sleep soundly. When a person is really exhausted though, he must have sleep. At a pinch, a man cat-napping in a corner of the cockpit can keep going indefinitely. Watch out for the dozing helmsman though and see that he has his safety harness hooked on.

Rather than enter tricky waters with a crew of sleep-walkers, it is better to heave-to and rest, with one person at a time on look-out.

Index